My Mother's Times

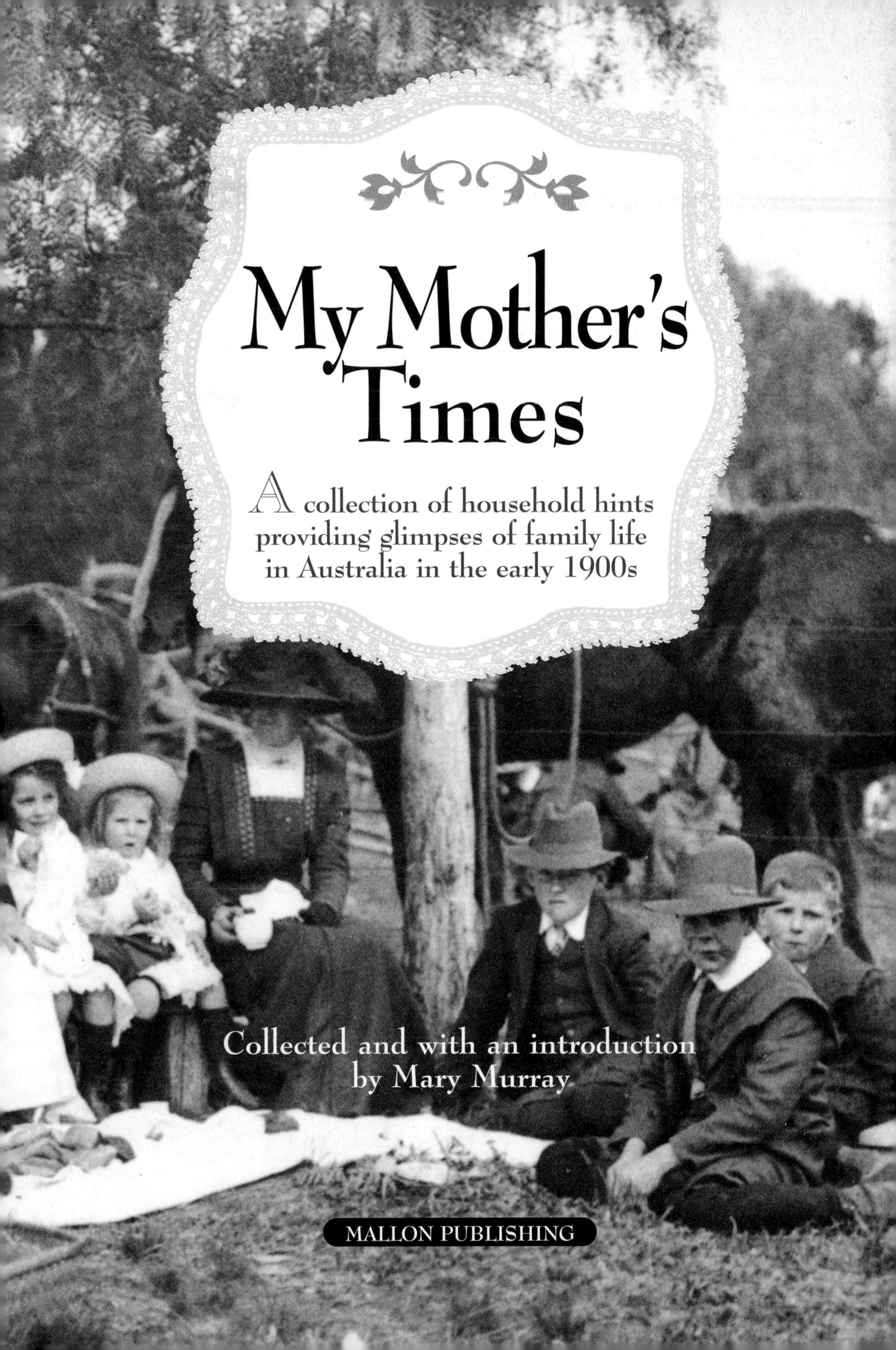

My Mother's Times

A collection of household hints providing glimpses of family life in Australia in the early 1900s

Collected and with an introduction by Mary Murray

MALLON PUBLISHING

Produced by Mallon Publishing

First published 1998 by Mallon Publishing Pty Limited
PO Box 390, Clifton Hill, Vic 3068
Reprinted 2001

Printed and bound in Singapore by Tien Wah Press (Pte.) Ltd

Design, layout and typesetting
Pauline McClenahan, Captured Concepts

Editor Jenny Lang

National Library of Australia
Cataloguing-in-Publication data
My mother's times: a collection of household hints providing glimpses of family life in Australia in the early 1900s.
ISBN 1 875696 06 7.
1. Home economics – Australia. I. Murray, Mary.
640.410994

Publisher's note
Hints and remedies are reproduced here for their historical interest. Readers are urged to take due precaution and, if applicable, to follow manufacturers' safety instructions, if they wish to use any of these hints.

Contents

Acknowledgements

Thanks are extended to the following individuals and families for their generosity in providing photographs for this collection: Peggy Anderson, Bessie and Ken Broadbent, Grace Coats, Nancy Falkenhagen, Mary Hickerton, Mary Murray, Valda Murden, Carmel Ryan, Rhonda Simpson, Janice Tunks, and the McDonald, Mallon, O'Brien, O'Connell and Rushford families.

Thanks are also extended to the Longreach branch of the Red Cross Society for providing a selection of hints and remedies.

The illustrations on the following pages are reproduced with the kind permission of the National Library of Australia (photographic collections indicated in brackets): 4, 6 (Humphery), 7, 20 (bottom: Ivy Deakin), 21 (R. C. Strangman), 27, 28, 31 (E. W. Searle), 32 (top: Mandurama), 33, 35 (E. J. Brady), 37, 39, 40, 45, 57, 60 (Grace), 62, 63, 64 (Grace), 65 (Mandurama), 66 (Mandurama), 72 (Bullivant), 77, 82 (Mandurama), 84 (Greenwood Gillstrom), 90 (Mandurama), 91 (Tilba Tilba), 99, 100, 101 (Mandurama), 111 (Wunderlich), 119, 122, 131, 133 (Mandurama), 142 (Mandurama), 152 (Tyrell).

The illustration on pages ii–iii is reproduced courtesy of the Government Printing Office collection, State Library of New South Wales; illustrations on pages 8, 29 and 71 are reproduced courtesy of the Bicentennial Copying Project, State Library of New South Wales.

Introduction

When the first volume of this duo, *My Mother's Ways*, was published in 1995, the response by a nostalgic public, wanting to learn how past generations had coped, was overwhelming. The wonderful reception given to the first book has prompted *My Mother's Times*, again evoking the vast, untold knowledge of a generation of women who had the ability to make do with the few resources at their disposal.

When I began to compile these books, it was a personal journey for me. I looked back to a time when modern conveniences were decades away, when the old meat safe and ice chest were as modern as things got and when manual labour, the sweat of one's brow, was the only servant to hand. As I worked, I realised I was opening a time capsule to a rich and relevant past that needed to be recorded, a sort of 'back to the future' package of household tips, hints, ideas, suggestions and ideals.

Many people commented on the 'window on the past' evoked by the first book, which took them back to their own family life when the farm or the suburban block with side paddocks was a far cry from today's lifestyle. The nostalgia contained in this companion book will again take readers back to a precious era in this country, the likes of which we will never see again. Women like my mother, who lived in that early part of this century, made good use of the ordinary and humble everyday items in their homes, often working miracles by their ingenuity and practical application.

In their day, the family was everything; it was women's strength and succour. This can be seen here in their household hints, and also in the lovely photographs and snapshots that illustrate this collection. I am indebted to many people for lending their treasured photographs.

In many of the suggestions there is a hint of humour. Although times were difficult our mothers could see the funny side of many situations, facing life with courage and generosity of spirit, always looking for the silver lining, looking ahead to better times, keeping a cheerful outlook, and tending their homes and families with love and devotion.

I dedicated *My Mother's Ways* to my own beloved mother and my sisters. This volume is dedicated to them too, and also to the farming women of this country, and to all the pioneering women who even today are battling the outback in isolated areas. We owe them a great deal.

That my mother's generation survived, prospered, advanced, and helped build this country is a tribute to these women and something for which we should all be thankful. I know I am. God bless.

Mary Murray
Scarborough, 1998

Special Times

In the old days the special times were often those spent with your own large family. Though it would be a happy day for everyone when a picnic was planned, for the housewife it entailed many hours of preparation. A hot meat dish was stowed in large billycans for quick heating on arrival; cold cuts and seasoned poultry were added, with plenty of fresh loaves, pastries, large slab cakes and cream puffs for all. But special times could also mean sitting quietly making small gifts or greeting-cards for family and friends, or playing lawn tennis on the court at the side of the house with a scrumptious afternoon tea to follow, or going to a local ball or party.

A wedding was a grand day for the family. The reception was likely to be held at home, with all the catering done by a small battalion of sisters, grandmothers, aunts and cousins. Bridal gowns and veils were handed on, having been carefully packed away, to daughters and grand-daughters for their special day. In the days when photography was less accessible, photographing the wedding usually involved a visit to a photographer's studio. Sometimes distances meant that this had to take place on another day, involving the entire wedding party regathering, dressing up again and finding substitutes for the flowers carried on the wedding day. Sometimes these were part of the studio props. We are lucky to have wedding photographs preserved from the past, not only for their loveliness, but also because they tell us so much about the customs and fashions of the times.

For the elderly needlewoman doing light-coloured fancywork or crocheting, a dark cloth spread over the knees lessens eye-strain.

If you need an easy-mixing, slow-setting plaster of Paris for handicraft, make it by adding ten per cent of vinegar to the water. Stir the plaster into this, not the water into the powder. When you need it to harden, add five per cent of table salt.

For the embroidery set. When doing fancywork which necessitates the use of five or six different shades of thread, here's a good hint that will enable you to keep the thread from becoming tangled. Keep your empty talcum-powder tin, wind each skein of thread separately round a piece of cardboard, drop it into the tin and pull the ends through the holes in the lid. This makes for a tidy work box and prevents waste.

When bright, fresh flowers are difficult to obtain, realistic and very charming ones can be made cheaply and quickly using dry gumnut sprays. Buy a skein each of red, pink and creamy-yellow wool (gum-blossom colours) and glue small clumps, fluffed out, into each gumnut cup. With or without fresh green gumleaf sprays these fadeless gum-blossoms are lovely for room decoration.

Mark the tennis-court lines with aluminium paint. This gives more resistance to weather. Saves time and trouble.

When going camping, there is no end of uses for an old torn sheet to take with you. It can be used for extra teatowels, dish-cloths, facecloths, hankies, bandages, and squares for putting under bathing caps. They can all be burnt in the fire before leaving for home. It will cost you nothing.

Put a couple of candles in the camping kit. A short length will be a great help in lighting the campfire if the kindling and wood is damp. One match will light the candle — thus saving matches.

English people love their gardens and the wonderful variety of bird life which inhabits the gardens, woods, dales, hedges and forests of that beautiful isle. We also love our unique wildlife, especially our laughing jackass or kookaburra, which so intrigues our overseas friends. If you are thinking of making a gift to send overseas for Christmas, here is a bag that will please. Make it a half-circle as shown, or a square. Both are nice. Use canvas, strong cord or even good hessian. Work the kooka in brown raffia or thick wool, with blue on the wings. Add some green leaves. Work the word AUSTRALIA across the top. Being a flat item, it is easy to pack for posting to friends or family.

Make this spirit-lamp stove out of a large-size shoe-polish tin. Drill holes all round the lid, fill the tin with cottonwool and soak the wool with methylated spirits. Put the lid on firmly and apply a lighted match. The spirit burns through the tiny holes, providing a splendid little stove for invalids, bachelor boys or girls, or for a quick cuppa when out camping.

A hiker's hint: rub petroleum jelly on hardened skin on the soles of the feet and the backs of the heels, then sit in the sun for an hour. The hard skin will come away easily, leaving your feet much the better for this treatment. Never hike without a small tin of petroleum jelly in your pack.

When Grandmother went on a picnic, it was like going on a royal pheasant shoot. Trestles and planks were taken for the tables, with spotless linen cloths, and serviettes a foot square. There were deck chairs to relax in: as Grandma said, a picnic was supposed to be a pleasurable outing, not an ordeal. Her food was something to be long remembered: seasoned rolled shoulder of lamb, rolled brisket with a golden syrup glaze, pickled walnuts and potatoes with mayonnaise dressing, chopped shallot-greens and parsley. There was home-made lemonade for the children and her rhubarb wine was legendary. To finish off, we had home-baked apple pie with Cornish clotted cream — a hint of her ancestry.

For a camping foray deep into the bush, cook a good curry and a fricassee of rabbit or fowl, so that when you arrive after the long journey, the billycan filled with the cooked food can be heated while you boil the water for that cuppa. A more appreciated meal I've yet to eat.

To stop ants getting into a hanging safe at your campsite, smear the hanging wire with vaseline. Ants will not walk over this and your food will be kept safe.

A bushman's recipe for damper, which some swear by and other swear at! Make a hole in some flour in a ration bag, pour in a quart of boiling water and stir with a stick until you have a lump of dough, which you lift out from the surrounding flour, slightly flatten, and bake in the ashes.

A bushwhacker I know said that when he cooks corned beef he puts all the vegetables in self-raising flour bags, as well as the plum duff or jam roly-poly pudding, and cooks it all in the same pot. He says the result is marvellous, and only one pot to wash. That's what I call saving time and trouble.

When grilling sausages out of doors — especially when camping — put three or more sausages onto a metal skewer. This makes the skewer easy to turn and the meat cooks evenly.

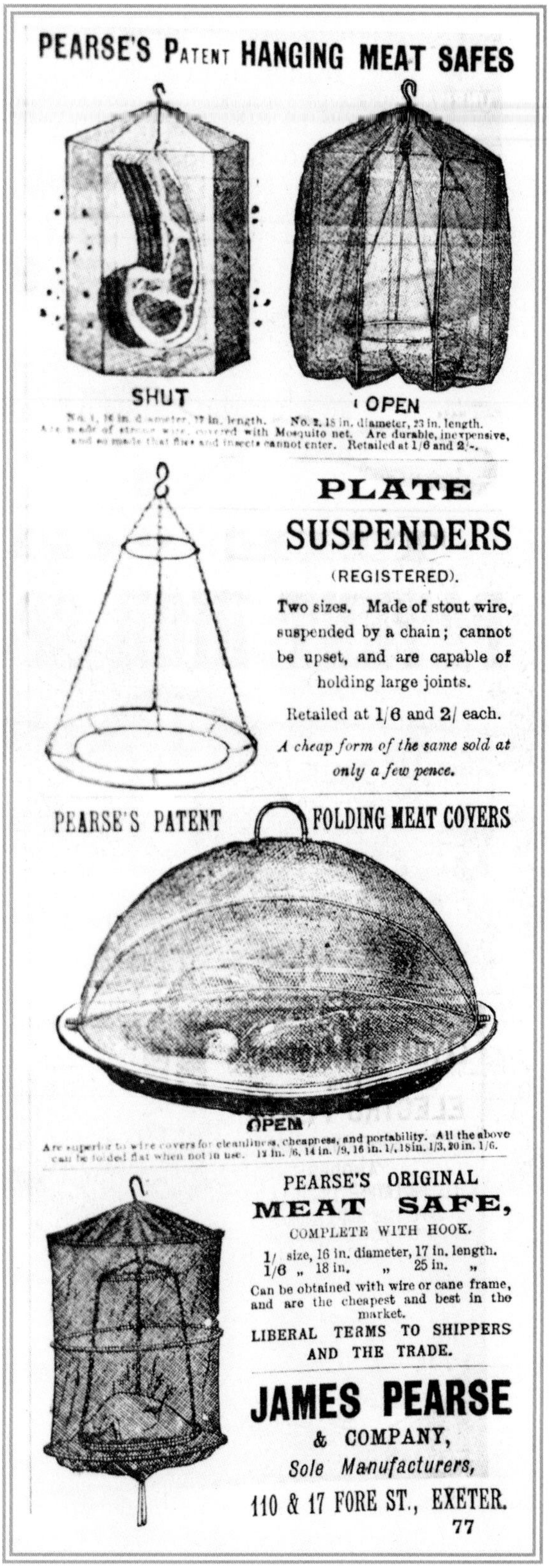

When building an open fireplace for camping, do not select stones from a creek bed; dry ones are far safer. Stones that have been under water for any time have been known to explode when heated.

Make this camp-oven steak. Sprinkle salt, pepper and flour over a thick piece of steak (or any good meat) and place into a pot with a drop of water and a lump of margarine or dripping. Put on the edge of the fire and let cook for a couple of hours, adding potatoes and carrots. Add a little tomato sauce to the gravy in the pot and thicken if necessary. A dumpling scone on top adds to the meal.

When sleeping out in the broad open spaces without a tent the rule is 'Feet to the wind'. With blankets well tucked in at the bottom and sides the wind goes straight past the sleeper and does not get down under the blankets.

After camping days are over, clean the cast-iron frying-pan by placing the whole thing in the fire and burning until it is free of grease and soot. This does not harm the pan and is most effective, fire being a disinfectant as well. Rub well with an old cloth if soot adheres and wash with hot suds. A bushman I know always uses this method, and I don't know a better way.

To set or orient a hiker's or motorist's map, lay it out so that the spot where you are on the map is positioned at your feet. Note some prominent object in the landscape, identify it on the map and swing the map until you are looking directly over the locality towards the object represented on the map. All other points will then be in their correct relationship to each other.

If you are the lucky one to own a car, keep the windscreen clear, bright and water-resistant by rubbing with raw potato.

Make sure to reverse the batteries in your torch when packing for the holidays, so that it does not accidentally switch on in your portmanteau, wasting the power you may need in an emergency.

A hot-weather drink prepared by the mountain guides of the Swiss Alps: to a pint of weak tea add a wineglass of light wine, the juice of a lemon and sugar to taste. Chill, then fill your thermos.

When the wash basin in the hotel room is without a plug, a penny will serve the purpose for holding water. Keep a spare penny in your suitcase always.

To friends going away by ship, give a bunch of flowers rather than a spray or a basket. Most basket flowers are wired, so they are useless next day and likely to be thrown overboard. A bunch can be put in a vase and enjoyed by many passengers in the stateroom.

Here is a good idea for a memorable wedding cake. Make a two-tiered cake with a hole through the centre of the second tier. Place a tiny ladder in the hole, leading from the first tier to the second. Stand a figure of a bride at the bottom of the ladder with a groom beside her, inviting her to join him in the climb to a 'star-studded future'. Decorate the cake with the usual horseshoes and wishbones in silver, with small red roses at each corner.

Identify your plate when taking cakes or other goodies to a party or the local barn dance by putting your name on a piece of sticking-plaster underneath the plate. It will stand dozens of washings-up. When the invitation says 'Bring a plate', yours will be ready.

At our local ball we had what was called a traffic dance. This is a variation of the well-known Monte Carlo. Mark two parallel lines down and across the floor (the distance apart will depend on floor space). Dancers within the lines when the music stops are 'out', while others in the 'safety zones' continue until only one couple is left. It's lots of fun.

This 'lucky' dance is a change for your local dance or ball. Let all the girls draw a slip of paper (sealed, of course), one slip being marked 'Lady Luck'. Make it an 'excuse me' dance, with the boys changing partners as they wish. When the dance ends, the girls open their slips of paper and the boy dancing with 'Lady Luck' wins a prize for himself and his partner. It's a dance the boys really enjoy: they get the girl of their choice *and* a chance of a prize!

A 'bird parade' is something different for a fancy-dress social. Each costume must represent the name of a bird, and (as a competition) players guess the birds portrayed. The soldier, parson and cardinal birds are easily represented; the honey-eater by someone eating from a honey-jar; and the heron by someone wearing a large wig of horsehair and showing long stocking-clad legs. The kingfisher wears a crown and carries a fishing-rod!

COMPETITION IDEAS FOR YOUR CHURCH BAZAAR

Wrap a book in plain paper, putting a visible marker at a certain page, and invite people to guess the page number.

Ask people to guess the number of spiky leaves on a pineapple.

A good competition for the men is to ask them to guess the number of pickled onions in a large jar, with the jar of onions as the prize.

Ask the ladies to empty their handbags and count each item, the prize going to the one with fewest items. Tallies may be as high as 140; so you can award a booby prize, too.

Try this at your next fête. A novel contest is to have the young men set a luncheon table. Provide them with the table, all accessories, and the flowers (not arranged). The result is hilarious. For the girls, try the quickest lighting of a set of candles. You will have many unsteady hands, and it will give the men a great laugh.

If a party fails to get off the ground because of shyness, or a number of the guests are strangers to each other, give your guests a pencil and paper and ask them to write down the funniest incident they can think of — real or imaginary. Read the answers aloud. The guest who causes the most laughter wins a prize. Laughter being the best medicine, the ice is soon broken.

Sell small shoulder-posies for sixpence each at your next charity afternoon. Wrap the stems in chocolate tinfoil (collected for the occasion). Put a lucky number in the stems under the foil, and at three o'clock draw the lucky number.

Loved Ones

The housewife of the early part of this century was lover, mother, companion and friend to an extraordinary degree. For the pioneering woman of the past her family was often her whole life. She saw to her husband's emotional and physical comfort and her children were cherished and nurtured through childhood with great skill and attention.

Large families were the rule rather than the exception, and a mother needed to use her resources cleverly. The hints in this chapter show how women directed their energy towards the happiness and well-being of their loved ones. Cooking, sewing and knitting were the skills most in demand, but imagination was important, too.

A sweet the menfolk will like: peppermints. Mix a quarter of a pound of icing sugar with the white of one egg. Beat well until creamy. Flavour with peppermint essence. Mould into halfpenny size shapes and allow to set. Dad will love them.

Rub in one tablespoon of sharp cheese to every cup of flour in a plain-scone recipe. These little savoury scones are much appreciated by the menfolk at suppertime after a hard day.

If very soiled overalls or men's working-clothes are put through the starch after the washing is done, they will dry more quickly and will be easier to wash next time: the dirt comes out with the starch, the starch having saved it from soaking in.

Men like their bath towels big, and most like them brown in colour and rough of surface. Save yourself a lot of work and buy them the kind they like.

A good shaving cream: beat in a large basin one small packet of Lux and one-and-a-half cups of boiling water. When the Lux is dissolved add one dessertspoon of olive oil and a few drops of perfume. Beat until creamy and thick, then spoon into jars and seal.

Degreasing hint: one for the men. If you've had some very dirty jobs to do, rub a little dripping and sugar into the hands, giving them a good working-over around the nails as well, before washing them with good soapsuds. This will remove all traces of grease and dirt.

A few drops of petrol put into the tin of boot polish now and then will keep it moist and add to army boots or shoes that extra polish that a soldier is always conscious of. Good for the non-combatant public as well.

When knitting children's jumpers a good idea is to knit a few squares in the same colour and wash these when you wash the jumper. Then if you have to mend a worn elbow you can darn the square on neatly. It will be hardly noticeable.

Try knitting a few rows of matching elastic thread into the tops of socks for about one and a half inches in depth Makes them self-supporting and does away with garters. This is excellent for children's school socks; saves fuss over broken or lost garters.

Two for the price of one. Make the children's dresses last longer and get equal wear all over by making them reversible. Buy material with no wrong side, then finish the inside to look like the outside. This means only a little extra trouble with seams and hems. Contrasting braids can be run down the seams inside and along the yoke and hems. This really makes the reversed dress look quite different.

Always save the material belts from old frocks. Cut in half, each belt makes ideal straps for a small child's playsuit, or can be made into braces for little pants.

If children refuse to eat their winter porridge, sprinkle liberally with hundreds-and-thousands. They love the look and the taste.

If a small girl is to wear long stockings with a fancy-dress for a party or juvenile ball, sew the tops of the stockings firmly to her bloomers and she will enjoy herself, because she will know that her hose will neither wrinkle nor fall down. Having to tug at her stockings will cause a little girl much distress.

When the children finally tire of the jig-saw puzzle, frame the puzzle and hang it in their room as a picture. Most puzzles are pleasing to look at, and you can appreciate them even if the children don't at the moment.

To prevent the children losing their spades on the beach, tie a piece of red rag to the handle; but write the owner's name on it as well.

Don't throw away a rubber-lined raincoat when it wears out across the shoulders. The skirt part will make an excellent waterproof sheet for a child's cot or bed.

If you are furnishing a room for a growing boy, use a travelling rug as a bedspread. It seems manly to him, besides having many other advantages — it's warm, does not soil easily, saves expense, and can still be used for travelling.

Odd pieces of leather-cloth or oilcloth cut into nursery shapes, such as rabbits, cats or Dutch dolls, and trimmed with bias binding, make attractive individual table mats for the tinies who like to sit up to the table. If food or drink is spilt, the mat needs only a rub over with a damp cloth.

When making baby feeders use a piece of elastic instead of sewing on tapes or ribbon. Quickly slipped over the head it saves valuable time, and it cannot knot, causing problems for both baby and mother.

Different kinds of baby food can be heated at the same time if you have a three-cup egg poacher. When the food is warmed, feed baby straight from the cups.

Make your children this delicious confection, a healthier sweet than bought lollies. Put through the mincer a pound of dates, two cups of sweet biscuit crumbs and one cup of chopped walnuts. Knead thoroughly, adding sufficient lemon juice to make the mixture workable. Shape into balls, roll in coconut and chill in the ice chest. For the adults, make it into a log and serve with either cream or custard for that special meal with friends. I tell the children they are called bonbons, and they love the name.

If there is a surplus of pastry after making the family pies, roll it out, cut into shapes with a small tart-cutter and fry it in hot fat while the pies are baking. Serve spread with jam and with icing sugar sprinkled on top. Children love these 'fried biscuits'.

Children's soft toys soon become very soiled. If they cannot be washed, they can be cleaned without much trouble by covering them with a thickish paste of starch and water. Cover the toy with the mixture, leave to dry thoroughly, then brush with a stiff brush. The dirt will brush off with the starch, leaving the toy like new.

Do not leave baby alone when covered with a shawl that has an open pattern. Baby's fingers can catch in the open work and draw the covering over the head. My sister, a clinic nurse in New Zealand, saved a child only by resuscitation after just such a happening. Young mothers especially take heed.

The taste of the nightly cup of cocoa will be greatly improved if a teaspoon of Saunders Malt Extract is added to it. A nourishing drink to give the children when they are going to bed

To lengthen a child's plain linen frock, join a two to three inch band of unbleached calico on to the bottom and another at the waist. Embroider little sprays of flowers and leaves at intervals on the calico in suitable colours. Greatly extends the life of the frock.

Save men's woollen sock-tops, cut them open, sew them together and make them into pullovers for toddlers. They look neat, are serviceable and their origin is virtually untraceable. If necessary, knit a basque, make cuffs and crochet round the neck. Made for church bazaars, they sell well.

If you are short of good wooden buttons for a man's raincoat, keep walnut-shell halves. Dry them thoroughly, then polish or varnish and drill two holes to take the cotton.

When making my husband's pyjamas, I use any left-over pieces of material to make a double half-back, from the shoulders to underarms on the coat. This gives the coat a double life.

Mothers, sew two backs into shorts you make for your children. The shorts will last twice as long, and darning is made easier, as you can darn one thickness to the other without much trouble.

Feeding the Family

The kitchen of the past was a warm and friendly gathering place: the place where the galvanised iron tub was used to bath the younger children; the first place you headed for. The kitchen drew you by the smell of bread being baked or scones just coming out of the oven, the aroma of the stock pot sitting on the back of the stove and the sizzle of the roast in the baking dish.

In very big kitchens two stoves stood side by side: one for meat and poultry, soups and stews, the other for breads, scones, pastries and slab cakes large enough to feed a shearing shed full of men. A treasury of home-cooked food came from these wonderful kitchens.

In those days meat was killed and hung, poultry was killed and plucked, and pigs were stuck and put on a butcher's hook, and all were cut up on a butcher's block. Without refrigeration, meat, pork, bacon and ham were smoked, cured and hung in vermin-proof rooms; other meats were pickled in brine in barrels. Meat was often eaten in large quantities and there was a much greater consumption of animal fat than we would consider healthy today.

Look for the tips that will help you in the kitchen — timeless tips that work as well as ever they did.

It is quite simple to make tough meat tender by pouring a little rum, brandy or other spirits over the meat and leaving it stand for about a quarter of an hour. In that time the alcohol disappears but the meat will be tender and appetising.

Keep a card of large safety pins in your kitchen for sealing stuffed poultry — fowls, ducks and turkey — and pocket-meat, such as steak. This is easier and quicker than needle and thread. After use, oil the pins with a little olive oil and keep them in a special tin.

To serve with crumbed veal chops, cutlets or steak, have you ever tried slices of grapefruit or orange, dusted with cinnamon and brown sugar and heated under the griller or in the pan? They are delicious.

A tasty topping for loin of pork. When the roast is nearly cooked, spread the top generously with apple sauce mixed with brown sugar and a little cinnamon. Brown until a crust forms. Everyone loves it.

After roasting the meat pour the last few spoonfuls of dripping into a soup plate or shallow dish and allow to cool. It tastes good spread on toast and sprinkled with salt and pepper.

PARAKEET PIE

1 dozen parakeets, 4 rashers of bacon, 3 hard-boiled eggs, pepper and salt, stock or water, a few sticks of beef (underdone cold beef is best for this purpose), minced parsley, lemon peel, puff paste. Line a pie dish with the beef cut into strips. Over them place 6 of the parakeets dredged with flour. Fill up the spaces with the eggs cut into slices and scatter the parsley and lemon peel over. Next put in the bacon cut in small strips, then the remaining parakeets and fill up with the beef, seasoning all well. Pour in stock or water to nearly fill the dish, cover with puff paste and bake for one hour.

A useful little gadget for scaling fish can be made by sanding a twelve-inch piece of wood for the handle section and tacking some beer-bottle tops at one end. When the tops become rusty, remove them and replace with new ones. Cheaper than buying a fish-scaler.

When frying fish in an egg batter, use a large flat pan (a cast-iron pan is excellent) and instead of throwing away the surplus batter, pour it over the chips and cook the lot together. Thin the batter slightly if too thick, and add a little more salt and pepper. Delicious.

Add a dessertspoon of vinegar to the fat for frying fish before it gets too hot. This prevents the fat being absorbed by the fish.

For something different to serve with fish, thick slices of cucumber browned in hot fat are nice.

Ways of keeping fruit and vegetables. Onions: the best way is to spread them out over the floor. Celery: bury in dry sand. Turnips: bury them deep in the ground and they will keep until spring. Lemons: keep covered in cold water. They will also be juicier if kept this way. The water should be changed every week. Cucumbers will keep fresh and firm for several weeks if rolled in damp newspaper and packed in a tin.

A North Queensland friend picks her mangoes before they are properly ripe and slices and cooks them with corned beef as a substitute for other vegetables. They are far better than swedes or pumpkin. The flavour of the salt through the fruit is delicious. The ripe fruit can be made into jam or chutney, crystallised or dried, made into fruit salad, or served with ice-cream.

If potatoes boil to a mush, drain, reserving the liquid for gravy or soups, then mix in a small pat of butter. Pile into a fireproof dish or pie dish and brown under the grill, or in the oven with cheese on top.

To prevent red cabbage turning blue, put a lump of sugar in the jar before pouring in the vinegar. The cabbage will be a beautiful red colour.

A salad of shredded cabbage dredged in sweet mayonnaise, with sliced fresh peaches, celery and prunes, served with cold roast meats or ham, makes a lovely cold Sunday night supper.

Cauliflower stalks should not be discarded. They can be boiled separately, sliced and served with lettuce and mayonnaise, or sprinkled with cheese and served with ham.

Onions are even nicer if they are sliced and boiled for five minutes before frying; they don't shrink in the hot fat. Use the onion water for gravy.

Sprinkle a little sugar on onion sandwiches, as well as pepper and salt. They taste much better.

A clothes peg, the 'dolly' not the spring type, makes an excellent kitchen tool for coring your apples and potatoes. Press both edges of the peg into the fruit and turn round and round until the apple is nicely cleaned for baking or the potato ready for mince filling.

A knife held in two slotted cleats nailed to a board enables you to slice potatoes, carrots, apples and other vegetables with considerable ease.

Keep that sprouting onion. Set it with a few other sprouters in a shallow dish covered with soil, and keep it damp. They send up plenty of green shoots which may be used to flavour soups, stews and salads.

When cooking an empty tart shell for later use, invert the plate and spread the pastry over the outside. Trim and bake in the usual way. Baking 'blind' this way saves the use of dried peas or beans to prevent the pastry rising.

Make a few small bags from either mosquito net or cheesecloth. When you are cooking peas or beans with other vegetables the bags will keep them separated, saving you time and gas, and using just one saucepan.

Apples and other fruit may be cored and cut in halves with the same stroke if the knife is fitted with a thin steel or brass cylinder.

A pinch of bicarb soda will keep new milk fresh for a long time, brings out the colour in rhubarb and helps to tenderise beetroot.

Save sugar when making a tart or pudding out of sour fruit by adding a level teaspoon of bicarb soda. The soda removes the sourness more completely than additional sugar would.

If there is too much liquid in an apple tart, crumble a slice or two of bread into the apples. It is absorbed quickly and makes extra filling for the tart.

To dice fresh pineapple quickly and without mess, cut it lengthwise and remove the hard core. Then with a sharp knife make cuts through to the skin (but not cutting into the skin), about half an inch apart in both directions, and scrape the flesh into a large dish with a fork. Every bit of fruit can be removed from the skin, with no juice wasted.

Instead of throwing away apple parings, put them into water and simmer until all the goodness is in the liquid (this takes about fifteen minutes), then strain and keep the liquid for your next jam-making. It not only improves the flavour, but also helps the jam to set.

Pineapple skins may be cooked with sugar and water, with lemon juice added, to make a good summer drink.

Rhubarb is better if cooked without water, as the stalk already has sufficient juice. Prepare rhubarb the night before by sprinkling the cut-up stalks with plenty of sugar. Next morning bring slowly to the boil. Takes less time and the syrup will be thick and delicious.

Have you ever tried setting cooked rhubarb in either strawberry or port wine jelly crystals? Use very little water (one or two tablespoons) to cook the rhubarb and slightly less water to make the jelly. Serve with cream.

Add a few dates to a nutloaf; a pinch of cayenne to gingerbread; a squeeze of lemon juice to pastry; a pinch of salt to whipped eggwhites; olive oil to mixed mustard; a teaspoon of coconut to curry; and grated orange rind to a fruit cake.

Two tablespoons of cooked sago or tapioca added to the mixture when making batter for banana fritters (or a similar dish) prevents it from shrinking away from the fruit, and adds to the flavour.

Chokos peeled, quartered, cored, stuck with cloves and stewed in a sweet syrup are transformed into delicious 'pears'. If you use half a packet of lemon jelly crystals and less sugar they are delightful — and no one knows the difference. Add jelly crystals when pears are nearly cooked, stirring to dissolve, and take off the heat immediately.

Use part water and part cold tea when cooking prunes; add a little sago to thicken. Makes a thick, rich brown syrup.

A tablespoon of custard powder added to every cup of flour when using a pale-coloured shortening such as lard or dripping makes all the difference to the finished cooking, whether for pastry or cakes.

A pancake secret. Once the batter is ready for cooking, do not stir or beat it again; that's what makes many pancakes tough.

Try using cornflour on your rolling-board instead of flour when next you make scones or pastry. It will not make the mixture tough if it is frequently rolled or kneaded, and it leaves the rolling-pin cleaner.

By putting one or more rubber rings round the end of the rolling-pin, the pastry for your pies may be rolled to uniform thickness.

For scones the oven must be hot, with a good bottom heat so that the dough rises as soon as it is put in the oven. The quicker the scones cook the better, within reason; that is to say the oven should not be at 'burning' heat, but rather at 'browning' heat. Each housewife will know her own oven best.

Instead of using a frying-pan when making drop scones, put the oven-slide on top of the stove, grease well and be surprised at the difference in the cooked scones.

When making a cake, put the butter and sugar into the bowl and allow to stand until butter has reasonably softened, then place a wooden spoon straight up in the bowl, hold with the palms of both hands and rub vigorously (like a fire stick). You will find this eliminates a great deal of beating.

When making your next plum puddings, increase the quantity and put the surplus mixture into treacle or dried-milk tins, fit the lids on securely and cook. The puddings will keep indefinitely. Re-heat when needed. Very good for taking away camping in the bush.

If you are using dripping in cakes, cream it well with lemon juice and a pinch of bicarb soda before adding the sugar. This is a good substitute for butter.

A hint for cutting sponge cakes. Always cut a filled sponge cake from the outside to the middle, not from the middle to the outside; then no filling will squeeze out.

To cream butter and sugar with a wooden spoon when the butter is very firm, dip the spoon into boiling water for a minute or so, and continue to do so while you beat. The beating time will be halved.

To add flavour to Christmas cakes, place the fruit and nuts in an airtight container, cover with brandy and leave for a few days before use. The cake will taste twice as nice.

If you haven't a large cake tin, make your next large cake in a cereal carton lined with greaseproof paper, or for a small cake like a bar-cake, use a cardboard box. The cake takes only half the time to cook and turns out much nicer and lighter. (Use with fuel stoves only.)

When baking a cake that takes a long time to cook, such as a fruit cake, place the cake tin on a layer of salt or sand on the baking-tray. The cake will never burn on the bottom, even in a gas stove.

Save the cardboard backs of writing pads to put over cakes that may be cooking too quickly. The cardboard is better than brown paper, which could crinkle and burn.

When you have something cooking in the oven and you are pressed by other jobs, hang a red rag on the oven door to remind you to check what's inside.

If a cake is burnt in baking, grate or cut off all the burnt parts. Sprinkle with sugar and cinnamon and return to the oven to glaze. Then cover the top with chocolate or coffee icing — and tell no one about the mishap.

When eggwhite only is needed, tap the pointed end of the eggshell, making a hole only big enough for the white to pour out. This leaves the yolk in the shell, which can be placed in an eggcup in the ice chest for later use.

An ordinary wire strainer in your kitchen makes an excellent substitute for a flour sifter. No need to buy a sifter if money is short; every item should have more than one use.

Advice from a baker: 'If you wish to prevent a cake sticking to the tin, never wash it; simply wipe it out with a dry cloth and it's ready for next time. Always grease with dripping and with the fingertips'.

If you have no icing set, don't rush out and buy something that you may use only once in a while. Instead, drop the pourer cap of a salt shaker into a cone of greaseproof paper, cutting the end of the cone so that the pourer just shows. This device will do simple decoration for trifles and cakes.

To save golden syrup or treacle, heavily flour the cup in which you are measuring the syrup. It will then roll out in one lump — honey likewise.

When making biscuits mix the dough very stiffly, roll into balls, place on a greased tray (leaving enough room to spread) and press out with a potato masher. Much easier than rolling and cutting into shapes.

No one with lemons growing need worry about not having cream of tartar in the cupboard. A tablespoon of lemon juice is equal to a teaspoon of cream of tartar in any cooking.

To preserve the flavour of home-made pickles, add a little horseradish to each bottle. The difference this makes is delicious, besides acting as a preservative.

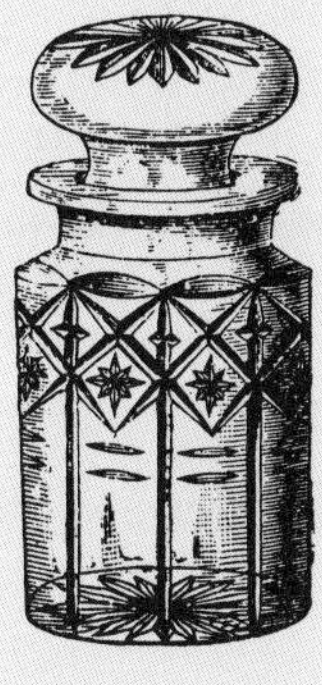

When beating eggs preparatory to dipping such foods as fish, cutlets, rissoles and croquettes, beat about a quarter of a teaspoon of baking powder into the egg just before using. The egg will instantly become thick and foamy, will hold more crumbs and will be a delicious brown when cooked.

Next time you scramble eggs, grate some orange peel through the mixture. More than one reputation has been made by this simple trick.

Scrambled eggs are greatly improved if you add a tablespoon of fresh breadcrumbs for every three eggs used. Also economical when eggs are expensive, and both husband and children like the extra body this gives the dish.

Eggs will go further in sandwiches if they are scrambled instead of boiled. Allow to become cold and add other flavours if desired: curry powder, celery leaves or a small onion finely chopped.

To poach an egg and save fuel at the same time, break an egg into a lightly greased cup or small dish and place on top of the kettle. While the kettle boils the egg will poach.

Poached eggs are delicious if celery sauce seasoned with a dash of cayenne pepper and nutmeg is poured over them. Serve very hot with buttered toast.

If eggs taken from the ice chest for boiling are put into warm water for a while and then boiled slowly, they will not crack.

If you want to boil cracked eggs, wrap them in tissue paper, screwing the ends of the paper in opposite directions. The eggs won't boil out of their shells. A good method in an emergency.

When boiling a large number of eggs don't drop them into the saucepan one by one; place all eggs in a brown-paper bag and put that into the saucepan. The eggs will get an even start; they will all be ready at the same time.

Hard-boiled eggs, shelled, put into salted, spiced vinegar and left for a few days — as many days as you like really — are very nice eaten as a pickle with cold meat.

Milk should be bought twice daily from the local dairy if possible. If no ice chest is available it is safer to scald the milk, using a double boiler. Then pour it into a clean jug, cover with muslin, stand the jug in a pan of cold water and wet the muslin, allowing the ends to touch the water. Keep in a cool, airy place.

Use this method to prevent milk tasting of turnips. As soon as the milk is brought into the dairy pour into it half a pint of boiling water for every gallon of milk, cover with a cloth (four times doubled) for half an hour, then strain and pour into milk dishes. *Note:* Never put a wooden lid on the milk pail.

For want of a patent milk-boiler, put a china pie-chimney in the saucepan when boiling milk. The milk merely boils up through the chimney and down again. No boiling over.

If you haven't a boil-over preventer, place an ordinary teaspoon in the saucepan when boiling milk. It works just as well as the patent variety.

When milk turns sour in greater quantity than can be conveniently used for making cakes and pastry, pour the thick milk into a cheesecloth bag, hang over a basin to drain and next day work in salt to taste. Return to the bag and hang for a few hours longer. The result is a firm, tasty cream cheese, or curd cheese. Very nice eaten with toast and cherry jam.

A teaspoon of lemon juice added to a pint of powdered milk brings it to the same strength as cow's milk for drinking and cooking purposes.

A trace of butter smeared under the spout of a cream jug before the jug is put on the table will prevent the otherwise inevitable drip.

Before commencing to churn the cream to make butter, add a heaped tablespoon of salt (free from lumps) for each pound of butter. The cream will turn to butter very quickly and this will save the hard work of salting later. Wash the butter as usual.

Condensed milk can be whipped like cream if it is first heated for ten minutes and then allowed to become quite cold.

Let us take a lesson from our sister housewives in England, who are being taught to empty drainings of milk from bottles and cans into a jam jar daily. The jar is kept in a warm part of the kitchen and the resulting sour milk is used for making scones and cakes (sour milk makes the best scones). A little vinegar will also make milk sour.

If you drop a large very clean marble (kept solely for the purpose) into the custard saucepan, the custard will not burn or stick. Take care to remove before serving.

Don't discard the square piece cut from a kerosene tin when the bucket is made. It is handy to place over the flame when the fuel-stove lid is lifted, and can be used as a fireproof mat to save blackened saucepans.

Bread-and-butter custard made with left-over hot cross buns or stale bun-loaf is very tasty and requires less sugar than when made with ordinary bread.

When making a baked custard drop a number of marsh-mallows into the pie dish. They will rise to the to top, melt and make a delicious meringue. A little coconut sprinkled on top also adds interest.

Fresh peach leaves give an almond flavouring if added to custards and other foods. Remove the leaves before serving.

To prevent a milk pudding sinking after taking it from the oven, run a knife quickly round the edge, allowing the steam to escape. This prevents a collapse in the middle.

Prevent fat from splashing when frying food by placing the colander over the frying-pan. The holes allow the steam to escape and the food will cook correctly.

To prevent the unpleasant odour of cooking penetrating the house, sprinkle a little cinnamon on the hot stove. The smell of spice is delightful.

If you have a gas stove, make one jet do the job of three or four burners. Obtain a tray (tin or thin steel) to fit the stove top, light one burner to medium height, place the tray on the stove and do all your cooking at one time. The tray will distribute the heat to all the saucepans.

Foods that attract ants should be kept in a safe. Stand the legs of the safe in holders containing water to which a little kerosene or borax has been added, or bind a band of flannel, saturated with kerosene, around the legs. A little kerosene should be poured on the flannel once a fortnight.

To keep flies away, place a few tomato leaves in the corner of the meat safe. Flies hate the smell.

A frilled-edge mosquito net for a cradle makes an ideal throwover to prevent flies settling on food-laden tables and dinner wagons.

The best bush 'ice chest' I ever saw was a two-foot square hole cut in the trunk of a big green gum tree, which continued to flourish although the hole had been there for a few years. Hung over the hole was a heavy bag, kept wet by a dripping tray of water which was filled each night. Even in midsummer the butter was always firm in this 'cooler', and jelly set firm overnight.

If a layer of white sugar is placed in the bottom of a biscuit tin the biscuits will keep fresh and crisp for months. Keep the tin airtight.

Keep an apple in the cake box. It will keep the cake fresh for a long time.

To keep salt dry and free-running, put a few grains of rice into the salt pot.

A tip for jam-makers. If you wish to make quite certain that your jam will keep indefinitely and in perfect condition, try this. When the jam is bottled and cold, before covering down, add one teaspoon of vinegar to the top of each jar and cover in usual way. This is a sure way of preventing fermentation.

Make yourself a bread tin. Cut off two kerosene tins, one near the top and the other half-way. The half tin can be fitted over the taller one, making an excellent airtight container. Lacquer the outside to suit your colour scheme.

A wire stand placed inside a bread bin will allow the air to circulate under the loaf as well as around it, keeping it fresh. Kept on a solid surface, bread tends to go sour; it needs to have air circulating around it.

If you bake your own bread or milk loaf, cut off a small loaf (or roll) and insert a slice of cheese in the middle of the dough after kneading it into shape. Baking will spread the cheese. Slice and spread with butter. Lovely!

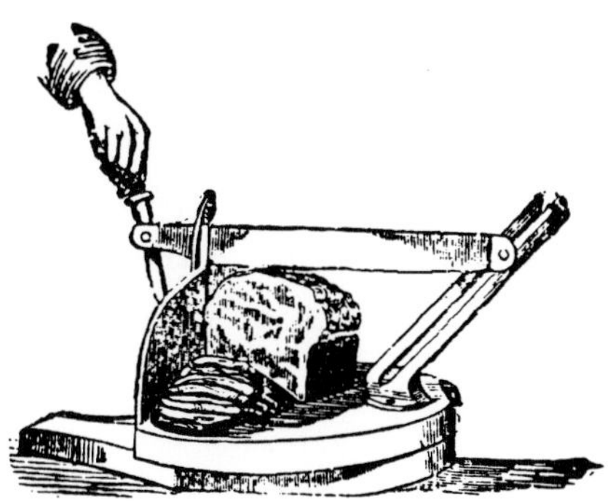

When using fresh bread for seasoning in poultry, add a little plain flour and you will find that the bread crumbles quickly and easily.

Try putting your morning porridge into a wide-mouthed thermos flask overnight with the required amount of hot water. In the morning put into a saucepan for just a few minutes to reheat and serve as usual with hot milk. A great saver of time and energy. Rice can also be thermos-cooked in the same way.

Use butter or lard wrapping papers for the top of boiled puddings; they will save the cloth from sticking. The wrapping papers placed on top of a cottage pie will help it crisp and brown better. Wrapped round a fowl, they will make all the difference to the whiteness and succulence of the meat.

Allow a radish plant to seed and become dry. Crush finely and use as a mustard substitute.

While mint is at its best, gather the leaves, wash well and chop fairly finely. Mix with enough vinegar to make a stiff paste, add a little salt and put into a wide-mouthed jar and stopper tightly. When mint sauce is required, put a teaspoon or more into a jug and add warm vinegar and sugar to taste. The resulting sauce will be as good as freshly made.

An ideal tea-infuser for making a large quantity of tea for social evenings, big outings or family picnics may be made by punching tiny holes all over a half-pound tin with a close-fitting lid. Only half-fill the tin to allow room for the tealeaves to swell when you add it to the boiling cauldron.

Did you know that half a teaspoon of white sugar in the teapot with the leaves will draw out the full strength of the tea? Use less tea (which is a saving) and note the difference.

If you are out of parisienne essence for making gravy, make your gravy colouring at home and save the cost. All you need is an old spoon and sugar. Put the sugar onto the spoon, hold over the gas or fuel fire and allow to caramelise but not burn black. Can be used for gravy, soups and stews. Improves the flavour too.

If honey has candied beyond use, for every cupful add a tablespoon of water. Bring to the boil and keep gently simmering for five minutes. It will be nice and clear again and ready for use as liquid honey.

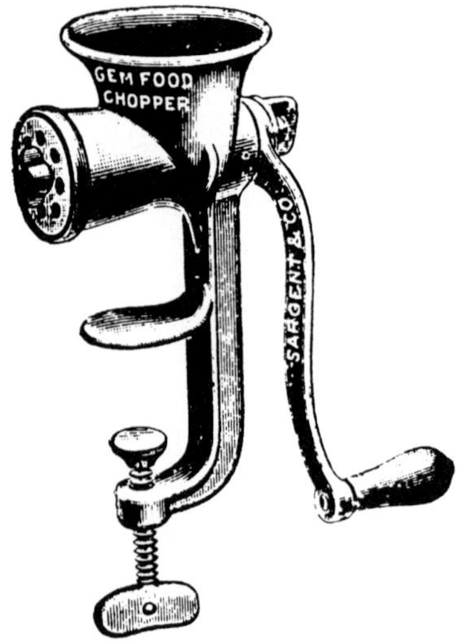

When the knives of your mincing machine become blunt, try this. Place a few scraps of sandpaper in the machine and grind them through several times. Then wash thoroughly with hot suds, and see the improvement.

An excellent substitute for a corkscrew is a screw hook of the type used for hanging cups in cupboards. This will pull the cork from a bottle in an emergency.

Paste a picture from a flower catalogue onto the front of an old telephone directory and hang it up in the kitchen near the sink. Pages can be torn out as required to wipe grease from plates, knives and forks.

An ordinary white bone collar-button stitched to the corner of a dishcloth is most effective for removing stubborn spots from pots and pans and has the added advantage that it will never scratch.

One fluid teaspoon	1/6 oz.
One fluid dessertspoon	1/3 oz.
One fluid tablespoon	1/2 oz.
One breakfast cup	1/2 pint
One ordinary glass	1/2 pint
Two teaspoons	1 dessertspoon
Three teaspoons	1 tablespoon
One heaped tablespoon sugar	1 oz.
One tablespoon fat	1 oz.
One tablespoon jam	2 oz.
Two tablespoons flour	1 oz.
One heaped tablespoon butter	2 oz.
One dessertspoon butter	1 oz.
One breakfast cup flour	1/2 lb
Two cups sugar	1 lb
Three cups meal	1 lb

A cupful of lard weighs 7 oz., a tablespoon of dry crumbs 1/2 oz., a nut of butter 1/2 oz., 8 large eggs should weigh 1 lb, and 6 lumps of loaf sugar equal 1 oz.

When a recipe calls for a wineglass of liquid, this equals two tablespoons. A gill is equal to a quarter of a pint.

A pen nib mounted on the end of a wooden skewer is a perfect measure for a 'pinch' of any condiment.

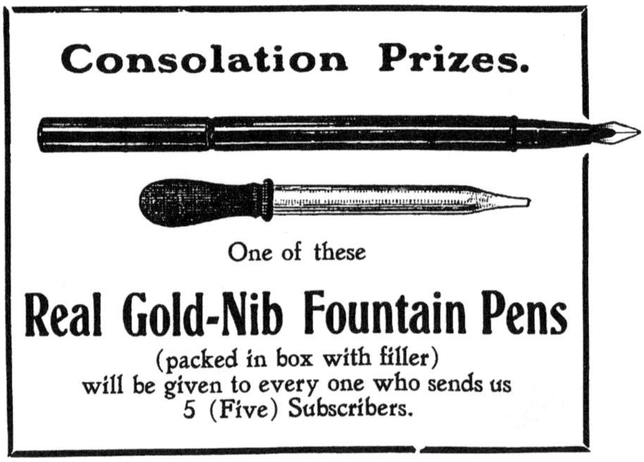

Furnishings with Flair

Furnishing a house in bygone days was not the simple task it is today when superstores cater to our every whim. Instead, the furnished home was an achievement of inventiveness with whatever material was at hand.

The mother of the family put to work her wonderful talent of sewing and making something out of almost nothing, decorating her home with calico, hessian and used flour bags. They were dyed, embroidered, appliquéd and otherwise fashioned into sofa covers, bed covers, upholstered chairs, cushion covers, floor rugs and curtains. Because money was scarce, everything was kept to be re-used, and given new life to brighten the home.

This chapter shows the skills of our forebears, especially the skill of 'making do' to achieve warm and welcoming surroundings.

Make a novel cushion cover. Children can make this and feel proud of their effort. Buy two mesh dishcloths and thread coloured wool through the holes, leaving the ends about three inches long to form a fringe. Draw a pattern to your own design in pencil or crayon and work in colours to suit your furnishings or bedrooms. Sew the two together and stuff with whatever filling you have to hand. Makes an attractive cushion.

When cushions become lumpy and are really uncomfortable, it is a troublesome job to take out the stuffing and tease it. Instead, open one corner and insert the tube of a bicycle pump into the filling, then pump until it becomes soft and fluffy again. Re-sew the corner in a few minutes.

Hessian dyed a rich red, green or deep blue will give new life to shabby chairs if it is tacked over the old cover with bright brass studs. It also makes cheap but quite attractive curtains for a bush house.

Instead of making pillowcases and cushion covers to open at the end, make a slit across the centre back, overlapping by about six inches to form an envelope. This is neater than an end opening.

When making cushions it is a good idea to have two or three of them the same shape and size as a pillow. Slipped into a pillowcase they provide that extra pillow when needed.

I re-covered my kitchen sofa and bolster using six sugar bags (cost one shilling and fivepence) and two packets of dye (a shilling). Now the children can romp on it to their hearts' content.

Excellent bathmats can be made from the best portions of a worn honeycomb quilt. Cut two pieces 33 by 21 inches, place one on top of the other and machine diagonally from corner to corner. Bind edges with colour-fast material to match the principal colour in the bathroom. Very absorbent and inexpensive.

Attractive breakfast cloths can be made from flour bags. Twelve twenty-five-pound bags or six fifty-pound bags make a cloth 60 by 72 inches. Remove brand names by boiling bags in a caustic soda solution (one teaspoon of caustic soda to a gallon of water), join with single seams (raw edges to the right side), cover seams with coloured bias binding and bind edges. Appliqué is effective on this type of cloth. It will last for years and improves with use.

Instead of turning sides to the middle in the usual way, get twice the wear out of your worn sheets by making the sound parts into pillowslips.

To utilise an old blanket that is nearing the end of its useful life, cover it with a soft material and quilt it like an eiderdown. With a little care a very dainty bed-covering can be made.

To darn a large tear in linen with the least trouble, dip a piece of net into starch and iron it evenly onto the back of the tear. Pull threads from the inside of the hem and use them to darn the tear carefully. This should make an almost invisible mend.

Casement window curtains will not blow out of the window and become soiled if small weights are sewn to each corner; and they hang much better, no matter what the material.

If you haven't a screen to hide the fireplace in summer and you can't afford to buy one, make a pretty one for yourself. Attach two hooks to the underside of the mantelshelf. Sew a curtain that will cover the width of the fireplace and reach to the floor. Put a good hem, a frill or a tuck on the bottom. Thread a curtain rail through the top hem and hang the curtain from the hooks.

By lining discarded furs or stoles with any strong material they can be made into useful floor rugs.

Have a supply of cheap barber's towels (cost about twopence each) and keep them in the bathroom. As they are thin, they are more convenient for wiping out ears than the ordinary heavy bath towels.

When putting blankets and eiderdowns away for the summer, drop one or two tiny muslin bags of cloves amongst them. Moths will keep away and the aroma is quite pleasant. Keep moths away from settees and armchairs by dropping a few whole cloves between and behind the cushions.

When an eiderdown is no longer needed against the winter cold, fold it neatly, put it into a bright cretonne or folkweave cover and use it on the daybed or divan-sofa. If used daily it will not attract fish moth.

If you are making verandah sunblinds for the fishing hut or holiday lodge, make a deeper than normal hem, sew one end closed and fill the hem with dry sand, then seal up. If a strong wind springs up there will be no banging as there often is with a board in the hem.

After putting aside my lace bedspread for summer use, I put a deep frill of poplin down both sides and one end of the eider-down. Besides keeping the eiderdown in place at night, the frill looks attractive during winter days.

Clever Clothing

In days gone by our mothers and grandmothers were needlewomen of necessity, having been taught from early childhood to sew, knit and crochet. A mother taught her daughter these skills, knowing that when she married she too would need to be inventive and practical.

Fine cloth was as expensive as it is today; therefore, 'Sunday best' clothes were worn only for special occasions. Everyday clothes were more often made-overs or hand-me-downs. For girls, dresses were trimmed to make them as pretty as possible. For the boys, Mother made jackets, shirts and trousers from sturdier materials and from Father's older clothes cut down. Winter garments were lined for warmth with flannelette from discarded pyjamas.

Hand-sewing preceded hand-operated sewing machines, which preceded the old treadle machine, which mothers of those days must have felt was the invention of the century. We can only imagine the time that was spent by candlelight and kerosene lamp, making garments for a large family, the work basket always overflowing with never-ending darning and stitching and materials waiting for clever hands to fashion something for growing children.

A useful hem-adjuster can be made by pushing a twelve-inch ruler into a square cake of soap. The soap is a stand for the ruler and it is easy to pin the hem to the required length while the garment is being fitted.

When buying material for coloured shirts, always get an extra yard. You can then put in new sleeves (always first to go) of the same material and save trouble trying to match the colour.

Make a double stitch every now and then when doing a hem by hand on skirts and trousers. It will last three or four times as long as single stitches.

If you haven't enough elastic to do the job on hand, eke out the length with tape. It is quite effective. I usually save perished elastic to help out with the new, especially on children's wear, so that it's not too tight for them.

When making your small daughter's cotton frocks you will find it a great saving in pennies to use all left-over scraps of material for hair ties and hankies. Besides it being a smart touch, the young fry will be very proud of their dress sense in the fashion world.

If a thread of cotton is knitted with the wool for an inch or so in the two rows before and after making buttonholes in a cardigan they will not stretch with use.

When knitting angora wool also knit in a thread of Sylko; this will prevent the garment from stretching.

When you make linen handkerchiefs and wish to do a crocheted edge, run the sewing machine without cotton or bobbin but with a larger needle. This makes even holes to crochet into and saves time in forcing the crochet hook through tough material.

Old celanese underclothing worn only in patches will keep the little ones in singlets. Crocheted round the neck and armholes they look quite nice and the children wear them happily. If your children are too big for this, make them for someone else's little ones. I did, and they were greatly appreciated.

If you prick your finger when sewing, soiling the article, mix a little starch with cold water, cover the spot with the mixture and let it dry. If it is not too noticeable, leave the mixture on until you next wash the article: the stain will come away with the starch.

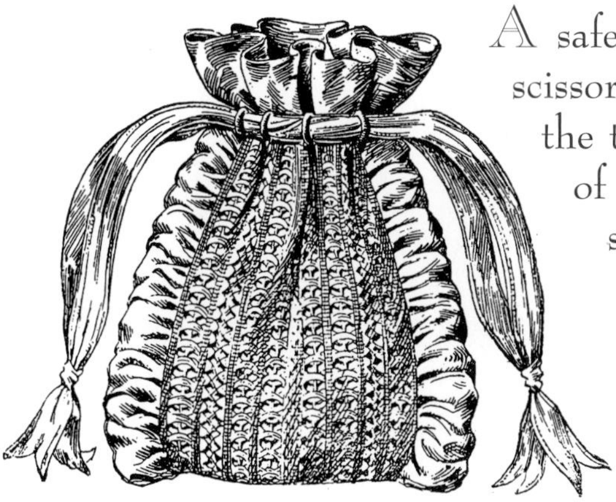

A safe way to keep thimble and scissors in a work basket is to fit the thimble over the small end of a cork and stick the scissors into the large end. The scissor-points are thus protected and both articles are easy to find.

Epsom salts sprinkled on furs and woollens will keep moths away and will not leave the objectionable smell left by mothballs.

To prolong the life of expensive silk stockings wear them alternately right side out then wrong side out. In this way the wear is evenly distributed.

If the heels and toes of your stockings are beyond darning and the legs are still good, make new feet with pieces of discarded milanese undies.

Make old silk stockings into shoe bags. Then screw small cup hooks into the bottom of a wooden coathanger and hang the bags on this. Keeps shoes tidy and dust-free.

To make new shoes less slippery, rub the soles with a slice of raw potato. Excellent for adults' shoes, and especially good for babies' footwear to stop them having heavy falls. If the shoes hurt, sprinkle talcum powder inside and on top of the wearer's toes.

To prevent clothes being rubbed shiny by the leather seat of a bicycle, thread a runner through the edge of an old beret, place it over the seat and draw it tight.

When the toe of a pair of new shoes or boots pinches, force a golf ball into the troublesome part and leave overnight. Repeat until the shoe is comfortable.

If your raincoat begins to let the rain through, spread it on the table right side down and rub with a lump of beeswax over the worn places where the damp has come through. Then place a sheet of brown paper over this and press with a hot iron. This melts the beeswax, making the coat waterproof again.

An old bush way of waterproofing boots, used frequently in survey camps. Fill boots with raw linseed oil, leave for three days, then empty out the oil, which can be used again. Let the boots dry for three days before wearing.

Kerosene will soften shoes that have become hardened through getting wet. This renders them as pliable as when new.

A bootmaker's hint for footwear that will not easily come to a shine is to give a coat or two of methylated spirits. When dry, apply shoe polish in the usual way, and see the difference.

When airing suits and coats on the clothesline, use two coathangers together and reverse one so that the two hooks form a circle when placed in position. This stops the garments blowing off the line.

Wanting a smart warm coat, I cut my faded moth-eaten cardigan along the seams, laid it flat between geisha silk and quilted it. A wonderful warm coat was the result.

A small curtain ring sewn in place of the inside loop of your coat will not break as ordinary cloth loops do.

Don't always reach for a pencil to use on a zipper that is sticking. Rub over with the end of a candle now and again — it lubricates without mess.

Any kind of old buckle can easily be coloured to match a frock by dissolving a small piece of sealing-wax of the right colour in a little methylated spirits and painting the mixture on with a brush, giving two or three coats.

A good way of securing a valuable brooch: insert the pin into a little bit of the dress, then into a small piece of cork, then into a little more of the fabric and fasten. A brooch fixed in this way will not slip out if the pin becomes unfastened. Tiepins treated the same way never work loose.

Prevent your headscarf from being spoilt by rain and save your hair from getting wet in rainy weather by waterproofing the scarf. Lay it between two pieces of waxed paper and press with a hot iron.

Fuller's earth rubbed into white felt hats will clean them well if it is brushed off after a day or two.

The cover of a black umbrella which has become faded-looking may be made to look as new by rubbing it all over with strong tea. Use a lint-free rag, allow to dry, and brush clean.

Next time you make a cotton house-frock, buy enough extra material to make an apron to match. Washed together, they fade together, and if a patch is needed the apron can supply the small piece required.

Items of clothing or any other articles which have bad-smelling substances on them may be freed from the smell by wrapping them up tightly and burying them in the ground for a day or two.

A fox fur should always be hung from the head, full-length. If put away in a drawer the fur is likely to mat, spoiling the whole fur for future use

A tip from a girl who is noted for being well-groomed and whose figure is the envy of many. When going to a dance, or any function which demands evening frocks, she dons a pair of long, wide pyjama trousers instead of scanties and slips. With these well-fitting pyjamas and brassiere her frocking is perfect.

TO STIFFEN COLLARS AND CUFFS

Add a teaspoon of brandy and a small piece of white wax to a pint of fine starch. Soap the bottom of the iron if it sticks.

Castor oil is an excellent cure for squeaky shoes and a good preserver for work boots. Stand them in a tin tray and pour in oil to reach the junction of sole and upper. Let soak for a few hours. Re-bottle the oil and keep for further use.

When crocheting edges to petticoats or undies of any kind, it is much more economical to crochet the edging on to wide tape. The crocheted edge will probably outlive the garment, then you can attach it to another.

In the Yard

The outside space was an essential part of the household. The whole family worked to produce food, either on the farm or in a suburban backyard large enough to hold people and animals in a comfortable space. Our parents and grandparents knew the importance of good fresh fruit and vegetables. If close neighbours were short on supplies you helped them, and a crate of produce might be dispatched by train to distant relatives. Father tilled the soil and grew the corn and chaff for his stock, while with the children's help, Mother tended the garden as well as bottling, pickling and preserving the abundance for later use.

When you woke in the morning it was to sounds of farmyard creatures all waiting to be fed by you; and they served you well. The cows gave you fresh milk, the horse your transport, the fowls and ducks your fresh eggs. Poultry was killed for special occasions, or when an 'old boiler' had outlived her laying life, this was made into a good, rich stew. As well as being agriculturalists and horticulturalists, our grandparents and parents needed to practise animal husbandry. Veterinarians were neither affordable nor readily available.

Our forebears' ability to adapt to the conditions of their day is to be remembered and admired by all of us.

To mend a leaky iron tank, mix equal parts of yellow soap and whiting into a stiff paste and fill up all holes with the paste. The mixture sets very hard and will last for years.

Not having a washer for my hose connection to the tap, I cut a hole in one of those cork seals from a beer-bottle top. A perfect fit.

An excellent emergency bag-needle can be made by filing the loop off a sardine-tin opener and threading the string or twine through the eye at the other end. Useful for sewing chaff bags or mending hessian.

When chopping wood, soap the head of the axe before using it. This prevents it becoming wedged in the wood.

Hold a red-hot poker on the head of a rusty screw for two or three minutes and it can be easily removed with a screwdriver.

Grandfather must have been a man well ahead of his time, because he used newspaper as an edging for his garden beds, especially vegetable plots. He used to say that when the vegetables were ready for picking, the paper was ready to be turned in as compost, to enrich the soil.

Boil rhubarb leaves for about half an hour, using about three pints of water and plenty of leaves. Stand until cold, strain, then water all cabbage, cauliflower, lettuce and brussels sprouts with the liquid. This will keep away all slugs and pests.

A lettuce plant grown in a flower pot with good garden soil and home-made compost will supply you with endless fresh lettuce leaves picked from the outside as the plant grows. It is also easy to keep the lettuce free of slugs and other pests. Grown like this, the plant makes a handy gift for a friend living in an upstairs flat with only a balcony.

To get rid of persistent weeds growing between paving and cobblestones, sprinkle liberally with common salt. Allow the weather to disperse it.

When planting out cabbage, cauliflower or lettuce, try dipping the roots into some liquid manure (just swish the roots around in the liquid) and plant the usual distance apart. This is a good hint passed on by an old Chinese market gardener. The plants start off with a jump.

Always plant a row of lettuces in between the cabbage rows. If you do this you will not have trouble with butterfly pests.

The best way of striking cactus cuttings is not to put them into the soil but to prop them up so that the ends just touch the soil. Cactus like to seek out the soil themselves, and in a short time the roots will grow down, taking hold firmly.

Strain left-over tea into a watering-can and use to water the cactus bed. This will ensure prize plants.

If your garden is troubled with little green grubs and snails, try this mixture: half an ounce of nicotine, one ounce of tobacco dust, two ounces of Epsom salts, two ounces of slaked lime and four ounces of soft soap dissolved in six gallons of cold water. Spray the plants, especially cabbages, with the mixture two or three times a week. It is also splendid for aphids.

Crab apples are well worth growing in your garden, as they make lovely garden trees and furnish a bountiful supply of fruit which is useful for making jelly. Granny Smith, who crossed a crab apple with another variety to produce her famous apple, is buried at St Anne's Church, Ryde.

To kill poplar tree suckers, spray them with mineral turps or power kerosene as they appear. No harm will come to the parent tree.

To obtain varied and beautiful colouring in hydrangea flowers, use equal parts of crushed alum and sulphide of iron. Dissolve in water and apply to the soil once a week in springtime, both before and during flowering.

Having a number of earthenware drainage-pipe halves, I turned them into flower pots by wedging in the bottom of each a tin lid pierced with holes, to hold soil and allow for drainage. Planted with nasturtiums they look pretty in the corner of the verandah or in dull parts of the garden.

Did you know that most gardeners live in the hope that 'what goes down must come up'?

For bald spots on dogs: mix one teaspoon of eucalyptus oil and one-and-a-half tablespoons of castor oil with sulphur powder and a little raw linseed oil to form a paste. Put on dogs' bald and mangy spots.

When cleaning poultry, dip the bird first into cold water before putting it into boiling water and there will be no risk of tearing the skin while you are plucking the feathers.

If you have a backyard chook run, plant sunflowers and Virginia creeper; the seeds from both these plants are excellent for fowls. Watch your egg production rise.

A trail of nasturtium leaves put into the fowl-run two or three times a week is relished by the fowls and is a marvellous tonic for the birds. You will be delighted with the extra eggs you collect.

Backyard poulterers will get a one hundred per cent clutch from the hatch by running a vinegar-dipped finger around the centre of each egg when setting the hen. The acid in the vinegar softens the shell, and the chick will make a clean, easy break.

When dressing poultry, singe it this way. Put about a tablespoon of methylated spirits into an old tin plate, set it alight and hold the plucked bird over the flame, turning it rapidly. Using this method the job is done quickly and thoroughly, and the flesh is not discoloured or smoked.

It is easy to reverse the car into the shed without touching the back wall if you tie a small bell to a piece of string and suspend it from the ceiling just where the car should come to rest. The ringing of the bell is the signal to stop.

Turn the paint tin top to bottom and back again every once in a while and save yourself the usual hard stirring process. Keep it at eye level in the shed.

Before putting away a part-used tin of paint, pour some melted paraffin wax over the top. The coat of wax can be easily removed and used again.

Avoid slippery ladder steps by painting them and, while the surface is still wet, sprinkle with coarse sand or rough sawdust. This gives a good gripping surface and makes the ladder much safer to use..

If your parsley has gone to seed, the soft flowering sprays make a dainty decorative addition to a vase of small flowers.

If a sea sponge soaked in creosote is hung from the ceiling of the shed the place will be kept free of flies.

For any kind of outdoor white finishing, mix ordinary whiting with skim milk or half milk and half water. I have also used three parts of whiting to one part of powdered milk, mixed to the same consistency as whitewash. The front steps and supporting walls have come smiling through some of the hardest downpours, still looking fresh as paint, but at less cost.

Epsom salts can be used to overcome magnesium deficiency in the soil. The symptoms are yellowing and curling of the leaves. Spread the salts over the soil and water in. For tomatoes, lettuce and citrus trees it can also be dissolved in water and used as a foliage spray.

On Washing Day

Imagine the washing day of the past, when the wood-fired copper was in a shed down the backyard, beside the woodheap for convenience. Paper-wrapped bundles of woodchips were neatly stacked ready, and a brick soaked in kerosene would be kept in a special tin for quickly lighting the fire under the copper.

All this had to be prepared, besides filling the copper from the water tank, preparing the starch and mixing the blue. Then there was the work of boiling two large copper-loads, firstly of heavy bed linens and white undergarments such as petticoats and bloomers, as well as shirts and frocks; then the rough farming clothes, and Father's grey flannels, which he habitually wore for fear of catching cold. The babywear, lace doilies and priceless table linen was mostly hand-washed. It was not an easy day.

These time-consuming tasks would stagger the heartiest modern woman, used as she is to her automatic appliances in a tiled and stylish home laundry. Yet when Sunday came, those mothers turned out their daughters in spotless white petticoats and dresses with pretty ribbons and white stockings, while father was resplendent in stiffly starched white shirt and neatly pressed serge suit.

In this chapter there are ingredients that can still be used. Ordinary household items such as borax, cream of tartar and Epsom salts, for example, are still found in our cupboards.

When there are tar stains on delicate fabrics such as crêpe de Chine or silk, draw the affected part tightly across the mouth of a cup; then, with the tips of the fingers rub in a little lard or butter. Next, pour over a little hot water in which a generous amount of borax has been dissolved, and with a pad of soft cloth rub just a little petrol over the spots. The entire garment should then be washed as usual. You may have to repeat the process.

Don't wring voile or crêpe de Chine undies or frocks after washing them. Hang up straight out of the water on hangers in a shaded place. As they drip and dry smoothly there is no need to press them.

After making soup, clean all the bones and save them for the copper fire on washing day. They burn well with an equal quantity of wood. Then put the ashes in the garden: they are good for the soil.

Where water is still scarce for washing and general purposes and you have to use bore or creek water, add two tablespoons of waterglass to a gallon to soften it.

An old country method of removing grease stains. Prepare a liquid from laurel leaves by pouring a pint of boiling water over fifty or so laurel leaves. Cover and let stand for three days. Strain and bottle, taking care to label the bottle POISON. Rub the liquid into the stained parts and rinse.

Here is a method of removing mildew. Dip the article in sour buttermilk, lay it in the sun to whiten, and then wash in clean water. Another method is to apply a mixture of soap, starch, salt and the juice of a lemon. Use half as much salt as starch.

To remove iron rust from linen and cotton materials, mix two teaspoons of cream of tartar with one teaspoon of oxalic acid powder. Wet the spot, apply the powder, place it in full sunlight for twenty minutes, then rinse in clear cold water.

When you are ready to wash men's cream flannel or serge trousers for the first time, mark the position of the crease under the cuff with a thread of mercerised cotton. It saves endless worry when pressing time comes.

Before washing your husband's ties run a tacking thread or two down the centre. They will dry and iron flat, and look new.

To bleach linen, soak it overnight in a solution of borax, warm water and soapsuds, then rinse in warm water with a few drops of ammonia added.

Buy an extra soap-shaker and keep your blue in it; then you won't have to plunge your hands into the tub of cold water on washing days.

A tablespoon of borax added to the blue-water helps to make the clothes even whiter.

To wash delicate-coloured muslins, make a thick corn-meal mush, salt it well and use instead of soap. Rinse in one or two waters. The muslins will not need starching.

Scorch marks on white linen may be easily removed by dabbing with peroxide of hydrogen. Then sponge with cold water and iron until dry.

To wash a feather pillow without too much bother, make a pillowslip from mosquito netting and empty the feathers into this. Seal tightly and swish about in a tub of warm suds, then hang on the line and rinse with the hose. When dry the feathers will be lovely and fluffy again.

Place a double thickness of brown paper between your apron and your dress on washing day; water will not so easily penetrate the paper, and your dress will stay dry.

Add a generous amount of borax to the last rinsing water for lace curtains. They will iron up like new and will be sufficiently stiff to hang nicely.

To those who have a lightweight wheelbarrow: place your clothes basket in it on washing day and wheel it to the line. This saves many a backache for the busy housewife.

Take the clothes horse as well as the clothes basket when gathering the washing. Clothes for ironing go in the basket, those for airing are placed on the horse. A time-saver, and fewer creases to attend to later.

Old and valuable lace should be washed by shaking it in a screw-top jar with a soapy solution. Then rinse thoroughly and roll in a towel to absorb most of the moisture before drying flat. Never rub or stretch any crocheted handwork.

This little portable clothes-airer can be easily made at home, and is a boon for drying smaller articles when travelling by sea or camping. Take two slats of a kerosene box, each about one and a half inches wide. Fasten these at right angles with a hook through the centre for hanging. Attach pincer-type clothes pegs to the slats. Once used, this handy little gadget will be taken everywhere, and is handy on the verandah at home.

Save all soap-wrappers and rub the iron over them before ironing. They make the iron nice and smooth, keep it rust-free, and impart a delicate perfume to hankies.

If your costume or your husband's suit has become shiny anywhere, place a damp cloth on the affected area and hold a very hot iron just above it, then remove the cloth and rub the steam into the material with a light circular movement. This will bring up the nap again. Don't place the hot iron on the damp cloth — just use the steam.

Blue-water left over on washing day is excellent for use when scrubbing the verandahs: it helps keep the boards white. If any starch is left, mix this in as well.

Make this household soap. Put six pounds of fat into a boiler with twelve pints of water, one small packet each of Lux and Rinso, two tablespoons of borax, one pound of resin and one pound of caustic soda. Add the caustic soda gradually. Boil for about an hour and a half, stirring frequently, over a very low fire as it will boil over enthusiastically at the slightest provocation. In dry climates, where soap becomes very hard when stored, the quantity of resin may be halved.

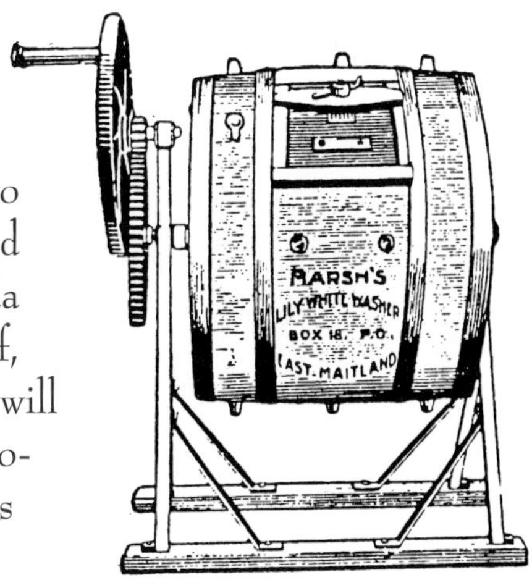

A faded dress may be made perfectly white by boiling it in water to which cream of tartar has been added.

Good Housekeeping

Good housekeeping is a skill like any other. In the past a girl was taught, not only at home but at school, by doing a domestic science course, which prepared her for what her life was expected to be. It was taken for granted that she would need this knowledge. At her mother's side she learnt the basics of good housekeeping while the boys of the family worked alongside their father, learning his skills and trades. Above all, the 'work ethic' was instilled in the young mind.

Much of this domestic knowledge was shared with neighbours, friends and other family members. The skill of being a good housekeeper and caring for your loved ones was a matter of pride. Managing the home well was considered a high achievement.

Old xylonite talcum-powder cases can be used as vases for posies. Flat ones make good wall vases. They look pretty if painted to match a room.

Make some charming 'filigree' vases by using up scraps of coarse lace or curtain net. Gum the lace or net around the outside of any ordinary bottle or glass jar. When dry, cover the lace with gilt paint, using a fine brush. The effect is like filigree. They sell well at fêtes.

To arrange pansies and other small flowers in a shallow bowl, pack the bowl with some fine foliage such as carrot tops or asparagus fern, piling it high in the centre. Pour the water in and arrange the flowers. The foliage will hold the blooms in place nicely.

A coat of brown oak varnish will turn a not-so-good glass vase into one of glowing amber, making it look worthwhile. A coat of varnish put quite roughly on a crude yellow bowl transformed it to look like some valuable metal antique, making friends envious of my 'acquisition'.

FOR YOUR FLOWER ARRANGEMENTS

Cold tea instead of water in flower vases will make fresh flowers remain fresh much longer.

Place unopened roses and carnations in lemonade instead of water. They will open into flower more quickly.

For flowers that are nicer in their appearance than in their odour, such as geraniums or marigolds, drop a couple of teaspoons of sugar into the water, and enjoy having them in the house for their appearance alone.

Small flowers and berries saved from old posies and fastened here and there onto sprays of green leaves make lasting and attractive table decorations when flowers are scarce.

If you wish to freshen up an old picture frame, a tube of gold shoe paint is as good as a pot of ordinary paint. My very old frame now looks antique, and I love it.

When pasting fresh paper on the backs of pictures or photographs, mix a little ground cloves or a few drops of turpentine with the paste to prevent silverfish and other insects from eating the paper or damaging the work of art.

A simple way to make a picture from a magazine look like an oil painting is to carefully cut the picture, place on a flat board, cover with cheesecloth and fasten down with thumb tacks. Coat with a thin coat of shellac. Leave two minutes and remove cheesecloth carefully. When dry, your picture is ready for framing.

If you are going to drive a nail into a papered wall to hang a picture, cut out a small triangle in the wallpaper and turn it back before inserting the nail. When the picture is removed the small flap can be stuck in place again without leaving a mark.

To remove grease stains from wallpaper try mixing some powdered magnesia to a paste with a little water and covering the marks liberally. Leave on for a couple of days and the paper should be as good as new.

Brighten up plain colour-washed kitchen walls by cutting out some flower prints and pasting them to the walls, afterwards applying a colourless varnish. They can be washed over if they become soiled, and indeed they brighten your work area.

Tan boot polish is a very good furniture reviver, removing heat marks and scratches. Apply a little on a soft cloth and polish well.

Don't throw away old pieces of velveteen. They are a good substitute for a chamois and much easier to wash. Use for polishing your furniture.

If you find worm holes in the legs of tables or chairs, fill small tins with kerosene and stand the legs in the oil until it has been absorbed by the wood. This kills the borers and preserves the timber.

Drive a large-headed medium-size nail under the legs of chairs or stools before painting. This allows you to paint right to the edge without bother.

Does the smell of paint make you sick? Try adding a teaspoon of vanilla to the contents of the tin. The smell is there, but dispersed, as it were, so that the fumes seldom cause nausea.

When cleaning or painting a room use a paper bag for a cap; it keeps the hair clean and is very light and comfortable.

Half a raw onion placed in an open dish of water and set in the centre of a freshly painted room will absorb the smell of the paint. Leave overnight.

To get rid of the smell of oil paint place a handful of hay in a pail of water and let it stand in the newly painted room.

USES FOR SALT

It makes whitewash more adherent; dissolved in alcohol it removes grease spots from cloth; and used with vinegar it will keep brasswork bright.

A MOULD INHIBITOR

One tablespoon of methylated spirits, one tablespoon of eucalyptus oil, two cups of warm water. Bottle the mixture and wipe on for mould.

Paint splashes on windowpanes can be easily removed with hot vinegar. This is effective even if the stains are of long standing; besides which, it deters insects.

Try this kerosene soap for household cleaning. To every six pounds of clean fat allow one pound caustic soda, seventeen pints of rainwater, four tablespoons borax, a quarter of a pound of resin (this may be omitted), one packet of Lux and half a cup of kerosene. Boil water and fat together, then very carefully add caustic soda. Boil two hours, stirring occasionally, taking care not to boil the mixture over. About a quarter of an hour before taking the mixture off, add the Lux and borax, and just before removing from the fire add the kerosene. Stir well, allow to set and next day cut into bars. Set aside for two months to harden.

The perfect use for those small pieces of left-over hard-to-use scraps of soap. Keep until you have half a pound or more, then melt them in an old saucepan with one pint of water and about a pint of fine sand. Stir until well mixed and pour into a flat dish. Allow to set, then cut into cake-of-soap size and allow to harden. Saves on cleaning expenses.

When having to broom out a very dusty room closed up for a long time, scatter wet tealeaves on the floor first. As you broom, the tealeaves collect all the dust and grime and freshen the floor. They are ideal as a first cleaner.

If soot should fall onto the carpet, cover it thickly with cooking salt. The salt takes up the heat and when cool the soot can be swept up without damage to the carpet.

For shabby verandah tiles apply equal parts of kerosene and brown vinegar with a soft cloth, then rub up with another duster. It is non-slippery and economical, and will bring up the different colours of the tiles.

To eliminate bulges in linoleum place a warm flat-iron over each bulge and leave for several hours.

When you want to freshen the stain on the floorboards around your carpet, rub with undiluted phenyl. It will colour all scratches as well as disinfecting the floor. When dry, polish with a dark brown lino polish. Doors, old heavy wooden chairs and tables can also be rubbed up this way.

Loose floor tiles can be re-fixed (temporarily or otherwise) without too much bother or expense if you mix equal parts of flour and salt to a stiff paste with a little water, and use this as a cement.

Don't wash linoleum. Sweep well, then dry-mop with a mop moistened with kerosene. This will keep away ants and other pests from the kitchen and bathroom. When polished as usual it will be brilliant.

To pick up fine pieces of broken glass, use a fair-size piece of cottonwool moistened with water. Every fragment will cling to the cottonwool. This will save you being cut, and the cottonwool can be disposed of quickly.

Don't throw out waterglass in which eggs have been pickled. It is a good cleanser, and may be used to scour wood floors and tables that are stained. Soiled 'working towels' or dusters boiled in it will come very clean.

Sometimes candles are of poor quality and hard to light in an emergency. If the wicks are trimmed and dipped into a little methylated spirits they will light readily. Keep an emergency box prepared with matches and a tiny bottle of methylated spirits in with the candles.

Boil new lamp wicks in vinegar, then thoroughly dry them. There will be no odour from them when burning.

If you use a kerosene lamp for lighting or take one camping, add a teaspoon of vinegar to each pint of oil in your lamp. (Do this with your kerosene stove too.) The oil will last much longer, the wick will burn more brightly, and the stove will give out excellent heat.

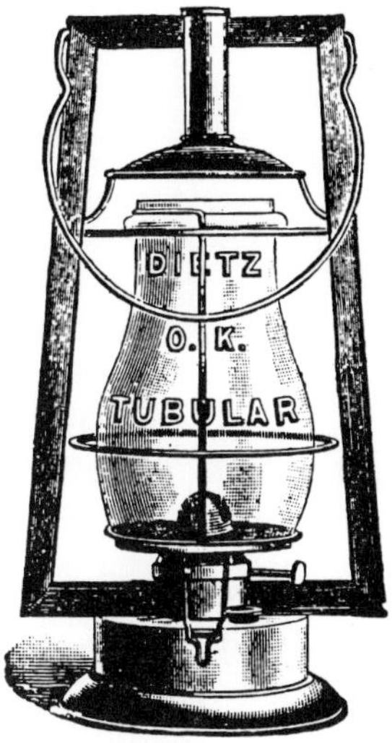

Save the corn cobs when you eat the corn. For starting the fire, soak them in kerosene oil. When needed, put them in the stove, set fire to them and add the fuel.

If you have to use screened coal, fill paper bags with it. Much cleaner in handling and so easy to pop into the stove.

Keep the water in which potatoes have been boiled and use it for washing silver, especially spoons and forks; it makes them bright and removes stains. Then pour the water onto the garden, not down the drain.

A few rosemary stalks thrown onto an open fire will create an incense-like smell in the room. It is elusive and very pleasant too.

To keep a cheery fire going at minimum cost, put three or four good-size lumps of pumice stone in the grate. If worked in with the coal or coke when the fire is set, the pumice will soon glow with heat. The pumice lasts indefinitely and may be used over and over again.

To make a polish for fuel stoves and grates, crush two cakes of stove polish and mix with a tin of ordinary floor polish. Apply with a brush and polish when dry with another.

This is an excellent cleanser for silver and plate. Boil an ounce each of cream of tartar, salt and alum in a gallon of water. When the solution is lukewarm it is ready for use; wash articles in it and rub dry.

Out of cleaner for the silver? Use a strong, hot solution of salt, and in another dish put dry bicarb soda. Dip a cloth into the hot brine, then into the soda, and apply by rubbing. Polish with a clean dry cloth.

Do not throw away the aluminium tops of milk bottles. When you are rushed for time, simply throw a handful of tops into a dish with the forks and spoons (but not bone-handled knives) and cover with boiling water. Let stand for a few minutes, moving the cutlery about so that it touches the bottle tops. Dry briskly with a good, dry cloth. The resulting shine will delight you.

Prepare cloths for the silver. One box of plate powder, one cup of whiting, one cup of cloudy ammonia, four cups of water. Mix all together. Soak flannelette cloths in this and hang out to dry. Wash silver in very hot water and dry with prepared cloths. A small cloth kept for bedroom silver is most useful.

Silver will keep clean and bright if you place an untreated sea shell in the silver cabinet.

After cleaning the brass use the duster with which you applied the Brasso to clean windows and mirrors. It gives a good polish in one operation, besides keeping flies and other insects away from the glass.

It's true that salt and vinegar cleans copper and cleans it well; but be warned, do not let it stand too long before completing the job, or it will leave holes in the copper.

To prepare home-made flypapers, melt together one ounce of resin, one ounce of castor oil, a small piece of beeswax and a little honey to attract the pests. Mix thoroughly and spread the mixture on lengths of stiff paper. Can be used in sheds and barns with great results.

Before you hang a sticky flypaper, pin a paper patty-pan to the bottom of the tiny cardboard container so that the flies fall into this if they drop off when dead. Dispose of it in the fire.

A good insect spray: one gallon kerosene, four ounces of pyrethrum powder, four ounces of oil of wintergreen. Mix the powder with the kerosene and let the mixture stand for two or three days, then add the oil of wintergreen.

Slices of cucumber spread over ant nests will cause ants to vacate immediately; cockroaches will gorge themselves into a stupor on cucumber; and if pieces of cucumber are placed near flypapers many a pest is caught.

Try this proven repellent for ants: dust the shelves and cupboards with ground cloves.

Give your bathroom a touch of fragrance by dabbing some of your favourite perfume over the light globe. The heat will release the aroma.

Moths will keep away from a piano if a few pieces of dry sponge are dipped in a little tar and placed inside the piano on bits of brown paper, well away from the wires. Tar, unlike kerosene, does not affect metal fittings.

Use kerosene oil freely wherever bed bugs are found.

Take a quarter of a teaspoon each of tea-tree oil and eucalyptus oil, a quarter of a cup of methylated spirits and four cups hot water. Mix by shaking, and use in a hand-spray around basins, baths and sinks. This acts as a disinfectant as well as keeping insects at bay.

If your bath is a galvanised one, enamel it with coloured enamel rather than white. Colours will not show rust stains nearly so readily as white enamel does.

Add a few cloves when making pot-pourri for the sittingroom, bedroom or bathroom.

When the screws that hold the knobs or handles on cupboards or drawers become loose, remove the screw and stuff the hole with fine steel wool, then replace the screws. You will have no more trouble.

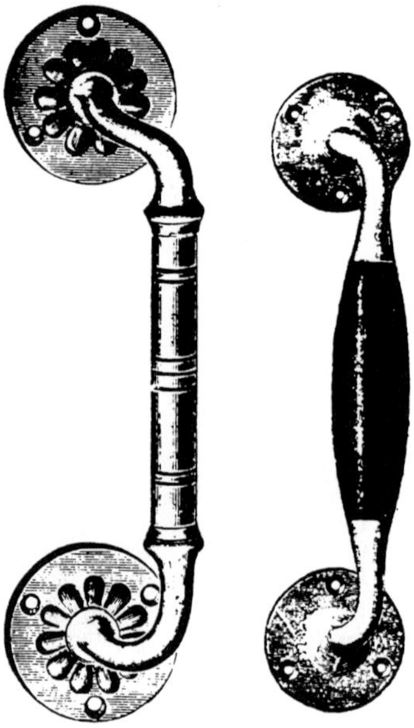

If a flush cupboard door will not keep closed try sticking a domed-head drawing-pin into the top of the door. Two pins work even better.

Nails to be used as clothes hangers may be prevented from rusting or damaging clothing if they are driven through a cork before being driven into the wall.

When it is necessary to lubricate any kitchen equipment (for example the mincer or the egg-beater) use either olive oil or glycerine: neither leaves a taste. Never use machine oil.

Any lime deposit in the kettle from hard water can be removed by boiling a weak solution of vinegar. The kettle will then heat as quickly as when new.

Discoloured decanters, vases and bedroom bottles can be quickly cleaned with a dessertspoon of rough salt just moistened with vinegar. Shake the mixture around inside the glass vessel and let stand a few minutes to allow the vinegar to work on the stain. Then rinse thoroughly with clean water.

To clean bottles that have contained a strong-smelling medicine, half-fill with warm water and add one teaspoon of dry mustard. Leave for several hours, shaking frequently, then rinse well.

When making up a bed for warmth on a cold winter night, put the eiderdown next to the top sheet and then add the blankets. The warmth value of the eiderdown is thus increased.

This cement will mend valuable glass. Soften a little isinglass in methylated spirits, add a little water and soften again by standing the container in boiling water, not near a naked flame. This forms a transparent glue which sticks glass so firmly that the join is virtually invisible.

Broken china can be cemented by making a thick solution of gum arabic and warm water, and stirring in plaster of Paris until quite thick. Apply to the broken edges and then press together. This cement, which is white, is excellent and will stand washing in very hot water. Leave to set at least 48 hours.

For the outback countrywoman. This paste will keep in hot or cold climates. Put into a basin a tablespoon each of starch, sugar and flour and a teaspoon of alum. Crush all thoroughly to a powder, stir in a little water and when thoroughly creamed add a pint of boiling water. Stir well and when cool store in jars and seal.

Rub fresh lemon juice into your cleaning sponge, squeeze through several times, then rinse several times in warm water. Lemons are great cleansers.

Ingenious Solutions

The most unlikely solution to a problem can become a world-wide success. Look at the simple safety pin: someone invented it to solve a problem.

In the past mothers and grandmothers, and fathers and grandfathers, were often forced to solve their problems with the tools or materials they had to hand. One has to marvel at their ability to fix it — whatever 'it' was: the leaking tank or bucket, the wagon or dray, the saddlery for the stock, the buildings needing maintenance.

Mother found clever solutions for the many problems that cropped up in her daily life, and invented ways of doing things without being told how to. Relying on one's own practical thinking just came naturally.

Many of the tips in this chapter will be of help even in today's household.

Open and wash empty flour bags. Useful for cooking boiled and roly-poly puddings.

Send eggs to family and friends in Britain by putting a layer of dripping in the bottom of a good square tin. When the dripping is almost set put in a layer of eggs so that they do not touch each other or the tin. Cover with liquid dripping (not hot) and repeat until the tin is full, then seal thoroughly. The recipients will appreciate both eggs and shortening in wartime conditions. Add some thin tablets of wrapped chocolate on top.

Another wartime hint. When packing parcels for Britain, fill up all the corners and free gaps with odd balls of wool instead of paper packing. The wool will be greatly appreciated and will make good granny rugs.

Give all the almost empty tins and bottles of polish to any needy bachelor friend (man or woman). It's only a trifle to the giver, but it saves an outlay of several shillings to the lone person who lives in a tiny flat and uses only a small amount of most cleaners.

When attending a kitchen tea for a bride, give practical gifts like a set of reels of cotton, packets of pins and needles, and a pair of scissors. Buy a clothes basket and put several dozen clothes pegs, and dishcloths and pot scrubbers in that. The new bride will be so excited about the coming event that she won't think much about all the ordinary things she will need after the honeymoon is over!

Instead of discarding an old toothbrush, remove the bristles, put a little fancy nameplate on this section, then shape the handle with a rasp to make a useful letter-opener for a Christmas gift. Always acceptable, and lasts for years.

A novel and very useful gift for a silver wedding anniversary. Select a box and cover it with silver paper, then cut a square of cottonwool to fit the bottom. Place on the cottonwool twenty-five polished shillings of the same design, evenly spaced. A little glue is necessary to keep them in place.

When you send out invitations to a kitchen tea, give a lead to your guests. The one I got bore this note: 'The kitchen is green and cream'.

A discarded shopping basket made of seagrass or straw can be made into an attractive fern basket for sale at the church bazaar. Line with bark and put in a good fibrous soil mixture for ferns or other plants. Looks nice on the verandah.

If your favourite flower bowl develops a crack and will not hold water, fill it with damp sand. Keep well moistened and the blooms will last as long in this medium as they would in water.

To mend a hole in a metal bucket dip a piece of linen, canvas or thick cotton material into cold-water flour paste, covering the entire bottom of the bucket. Bake it on top of the fuel stove until the paste dries hard. The patch will last and last.

To clean galvanised tubs or buckets make a paste of plain flour and cold water, add boiling water, and while the paste is hot coat the inside of the bucket thinly. Dry in the sun. The paste will easily peel off, leaving the bucket or tub as new.

When a dressing-table drawer sticks badly, take it out, turn it upside down and push drawing pins into the runners (two to each side should do). Then rub a cake of soap along the runners inside the cabinet. The drawer will run silently along the dome heads of the pins and require no further attention.

If the kitchen table is too low for comfort and gives you a backache when working, fix rubber doorstops to the legs; they will not only raise the table height, but prevent it moving about on a slippery floor.

When flies are numerous, three-parts fill a jar with soapy water and place a lid or a round of cardboard on top with a central hole in it. On the underside of the lid smear syrup, keeping it just clear of the hole. This is cheaper then flypapers and destroys myriads of flies. Clean and refill as required. Place some jars outside as well.

As effective as any hot-water bottle is a hot sandbag. Make strong bags about the size of hot-water bags, fill with clean sand, place heatproof mats in the hot oven and put in the sandbags, leaving the oven door open. When warmed, slip each bag into a soft flannel cover and put into the beds. No danger of scalding, and they will keep warm for hours.

If the evening meal has been cooked in the oven, put the hot oven-slide in a paper hatbag as soon as the oven is empty, and slip the bag between the sheets. Better than a hot-water bottle or a brick.

A novel and useful wool-winder can be made with two very large reels such as a shoemaker's thread is wound on. Put the reels about 24 inches apart on long nails driven into a heavy board. Put the skein on the wheels, which will revolve as you wind.

A soap-shaver can be made by nailing a bottle cap onto the end of a piece of broomstick. By holding the soap in the left hand and drawing the tool along it you can reduce a bar of soap to fine shavings in a few minutes.

I made myself a safe wallet a trifle larger than a £1 note. I used strong washable material and designed the wallet with a fold-over flap like an envelope. I wear it tied around my leg above the knee. An elastic band keeps it doubly secure.

Attach your latch-key to a length of tape and fasten it to the lining of your handbag with a safety-pin. The key can be found without fumbling and the door unlocked without removing the pin.

Try this to waterproof the ink on parcels being sent to soldiers. When the ink is quite dry run a slightly warmed candle over the writing, spreading a thin layer which will be transparent and will withstand wetting and not smudge.

If you live in an isolated area and lamp glasses are hard to get, an ordinary large glass tumbler with the bottom cut off can be used with success. The glass is cut this way. Tie a piece of string saturated with kerosene round the bottom of the glass, then set the string alight. As soon as the flame dies down, plunge the glass into cold water. It should crack where the string was tied. You can make tumblers or glasses the same way from any type of bottle. Smooth the cut edges with coarse sandpaper first, then fine glass paper. Decorate with a motif if desired. Very practical and a good hobby.

When the door-key will not work smoothly in the lock, rub over with vaseline. Insert in the lock and turn several times. Grease will penetrate parts you cannot hope to reach otherwise.

Writing the address on a large brown-paper parcel can be done very swiftly by dipping a matchstick in the ink and writing with that. The address will be beautifully clear and the postman will find his work easier.

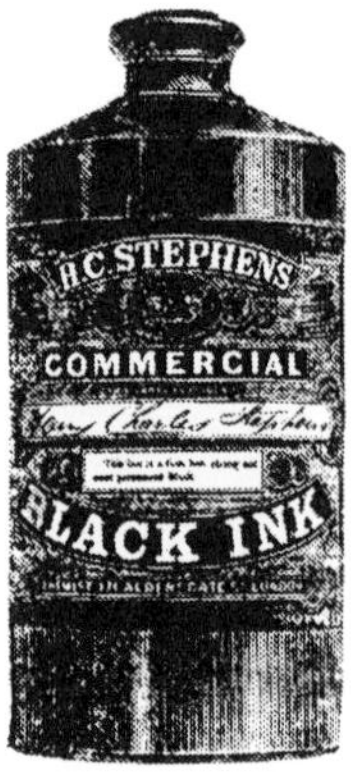

Make a recipe book for your friends by buying a small hard-cover book with blank pages and filling it with all the recipes they have enjoyed while visiting you. Cover it with wallpaper and give it for Christmas or a birthday. A most useful gift.

When receiving any mail sent in unsealed envelopes, cut the gummed strips from the envelopes and use them as labels for jam and chutney jars. This is easy and economical.

When you spoil a stamped envelope, keep it until you use an egg, them remove the stamp with water and stick the stamp with eggwhite to the new envelope. As good as glue.

Having upset a kerosene lamp over a borrowed book, I was aghast at the accident, but quickly sprinkled the pages with flour, wrapped the book in a well-floured cloth and put it away for two days. When the flour was removed there was not a trace of kerosene visible. I confessed my sin to the owner; the book was preserved for years.

If there is no clock in sight of the telephone, have a three-minute egg-timer fixed to the wall. If you are making a trunk call this will save you money.

If your alarm clocks rings too loudly try fitting an elastic band or thick rubber band round the bell. The band will deaden the sound. The wider the band the softer the bell.

A sixpenny bicycle bell, mounted on a circular piece of timber and screwed to the front door, makes an efficient doorbell which can be heard in the backyard.

Don't dig too deep a hole for the outside lavatory. Instead, make shallower holes and make a portable house with handles that can be lifted and carried to another spot. In time, plough and plant the area where the human manure has lain, and watch the result. Far better than animal manure.

For the occasion when seating is scarce, such as outback picnic races or farming get-togethers, try painting four-gallon kerosene tins and fitting the tops with cushions covered in a floral cotton material. Allow a frill about six inches deep on the cushions. These seats can be stored away and used year after year.

To moisten glue that has become hard and dry, add a trickle of vinegar to the jar and stir; it will make the glue liquid again.

If glue is needed and none is handy, melt a little gelatine in boiling water. Re-heat if it sets during use, and keep for further use.

To temporarily mend a broken umbrella rib, place a two-inch nail along the rib and bind in place with adhesive tape. This prevents the broken end from tearing the cloth until it can be mended properly.

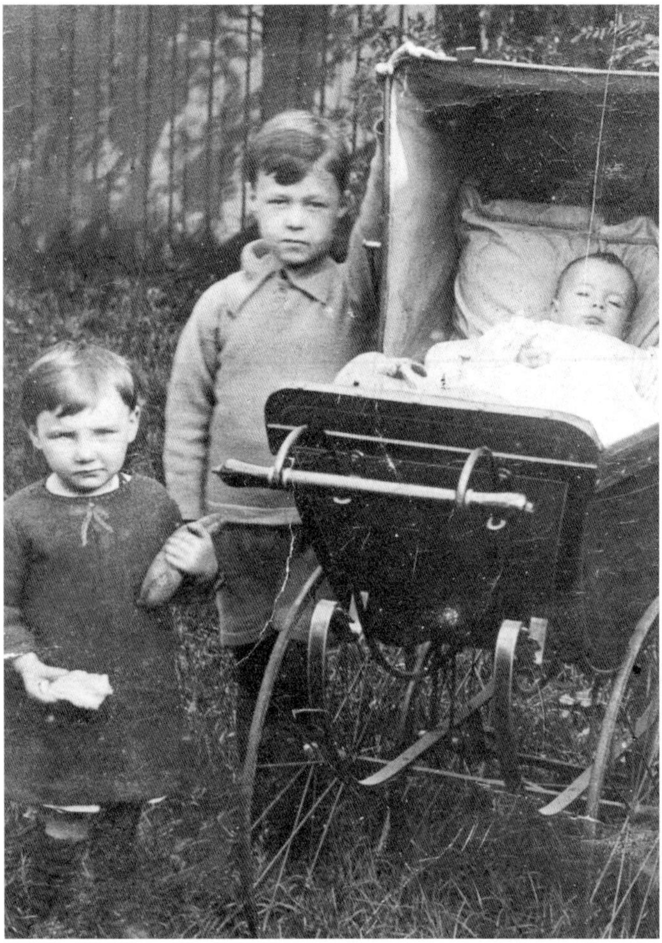

I saw the hood of an old perambulator put to novel use. It was attached to a deck chair in such a way that it could be adjusted to any angle for shade. If you dislike the dark colour, cover it with a bright striped canvas or heavy cretonne. Good for the beach.

Dry coffee grounds need not be flushed away; either throw them into the garden or use them to stuff pincushions. The coffee grounds will keep the pins and needles from going rusty.

Body and Soul

With arduous tasks to be ever undertaken in her life, the housewife of the past had little time to spend on herself — and no money to waste on luxury items for her own use even had they been available. Recipes for facial lotions, cleansing liquids and softening mixtures were passed on through the generations, with new ingredients being added as they became known and their properties recognised.

Well-known and well-tried formulas are still used today as we rediscover how our grandmothers kept their skin from being ravaged by an unforgiving climate. They used what they had to hand: oatmeal, starch, olive oil and eggwhite.

This chapter contains many suggestions for everyday health: first aid for feet and hands, a healing soap of honey, simple remedies for a cough or sore throat, and hints for the care of the sick.

HONEY SOAP

Just the thing for sore, chafed and cracked hands in winter. Shred one pound of pure soap into an old saucepan with just enough water to prevent burning, add a quarter of a pound of honey, one ounce of glycerine, two tablespoons of fine oatmeal and a few drops of perfume. Stir until soap is dissolved, and boil for three minutes. Pour into wet moulds (old tobacco tins are just the thing). Store until hard.

Sprinkled into shoes, fuller's earth gives relief to tired feet. It may also be used as a toilet powder (it is the basis of many) and is good for chafing.

A cake of camphor ground and dissolved in a bottle of methylated spirits is an excellent remedy for tired feet. Rub in at night. Keep the mixture away from flames.

The white of an egg has many uses. Rub blistered heels with it and feel it remove the soreness. Prevent further trouble by rubbing the heels nightly with methylated spirits; this tends to harden the skin against blistering.

For tender feet, mix equal parts of methylated spirits and olive oil and rub well into the feet at least twice a week at bedtime. Helps the nails as well.

My grandmother had an excellent remedy for hands roughened by household chores or a day in the garden patch. She poured a little castor oil into her palms, sprinkled on a little sugar and salt and massaged the mixture into her hands. Even in old age her skin was beautifully smooth and white.

If you suffer with corns, try this. Mix equal parts of glycerine and methylated spirits and rub into the feet morning and night. It will help banish corns, calluses and even bunions if persevered with — but persevere you must.

Grandad was a great walker. He attributed his healthy feet to the fact that every morning after his ablutions he soaped them well, between the toes and the soles especially, and let the moist soap dry on his feet. As he constantly walked from Moss Vale to Bowral and back, I think he had a point.

To promote the growth of hair take equal quantities of olive oil and spirit of rosemary, and a few drops of oil of nutmeg. Mix the ingredients together. Rub the roots of the hair every night with a little of this liniment and the growth will very soon noticeably increase. When illness is the cause of the loss of hair, brandy should be applied three times a week and cold cream on the alternate nights.

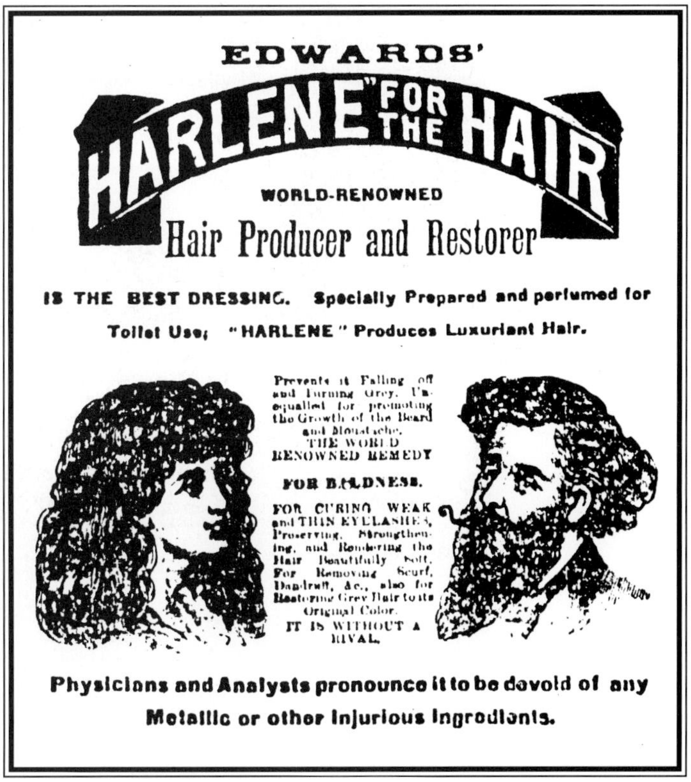

If you suffer from dandruff, gather a good handful of leaves from the lemon tree, cover with water and boil the mixture for half an hour. Strain and bottle. When it is cool, rub the liquid into the scalp. Even the most stubborn dandruff will respond to this. It's a natural remedy.

To relieve tired feet and keep them cool in hot weather, put some fine oatmeal into stockings or socks each morning. The powder in the oatmeal is beneficial to the feet.

Keep your quince seeds this season! Try dampening the hair with water in which some bruised seeds have been steeped. Pinch the waves into place between the fingers while the hair dries. It will kink nicely. This liquid is quite harmless and washes out easily, leaving the hair soft.

Did you know that the Chinese recommend watermelon to aid the kidneys? Besides being a delicious fruit to eat, the watery substance is medicinal and curative. What a happy way to keep oneself healthy!

Use a solution of salt and water to soak your new toothbrush. It will keep the bristles firm much longer. Do this once a week to freshen the brush. This in turn helps the teeth.

If you are unable to wash your hair — for example because of sickness — tie a piece of clean muslin over the hairbrush and brush your hair vigorously, parting it in several places and using fresh muslin as each piece becomes soiled. (An old silk stocking is just as good).

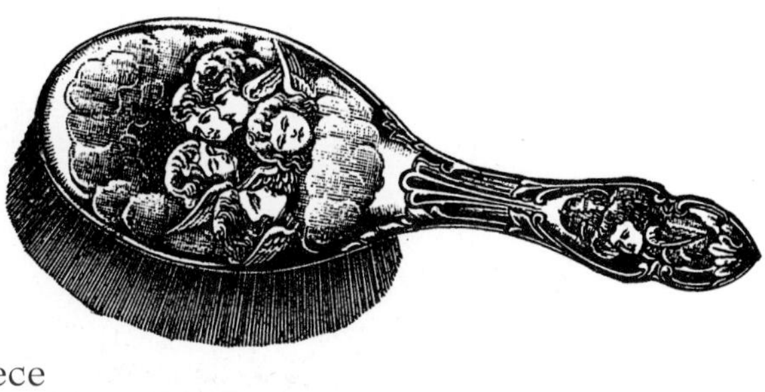

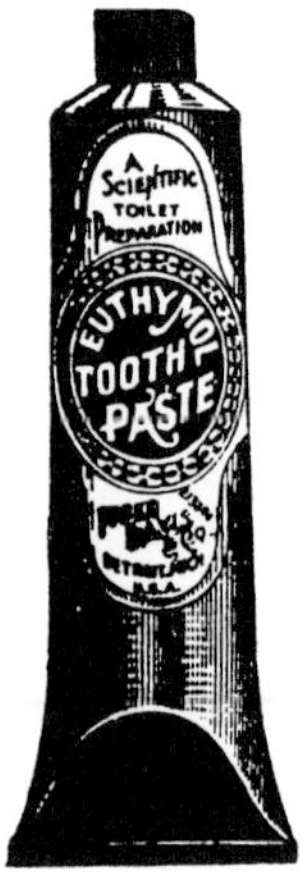

Salt will clean teeth just as effectively as a high-priced toothpaste, and also prevents gumboils and heals ulcers of the mouth.

Keep oil of cloves in the medicine chest in case of toothache. Soak a wad of cottonwool in the solution and press into the affected area. A good temporary measure.

A good way to clean false teeth: rub the toothbrush on the soap you use, and lather the teeth well before rinsing them thoroughly.

When teeth break off your dental plate, fill the cavity with chewing gum and avoid unpleasant soreness of the lips or mouth until you can visit a dentist.

A cupful of vinegar added to a plunge bath after strenuous exercise will be found to be very refreshing; it takes away all stiffness.

Keep a soap-saver in your bathroom for all the tail-ends of the toilet soap, and use it to make a foam when you have a bath. You can't afford to waste it.

Instead of using sticking-plaster on a conspicuous blemish, use the skin inside the shell of a raw egg. It adheres firmly, does not soil, washes off easily and is not nearly so noticeable as plaster. Being transparent, it hardly shows.

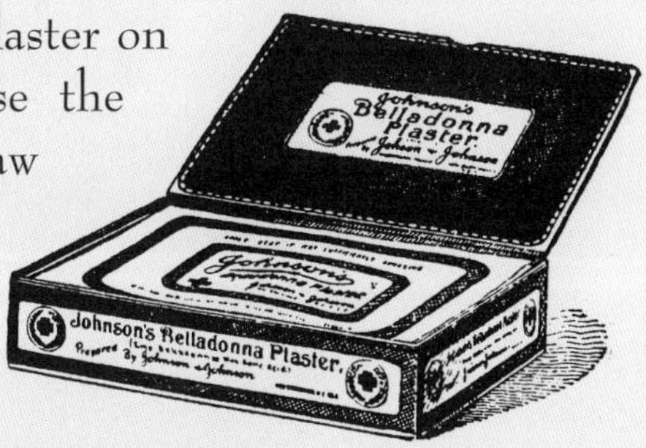

Over the face-powder in your powder-bowl place a layer of cheesecloth. It acts as a sifter and prevents the usual wasteful shower of powder which occurs when the puff is placed on the uncovered powder.

Did you know that starch makes a good beauty mask? For a normal skin mix the starch with cold cream and milk; for an oily skin mix with eggwhite and milk to tighten the pores; for a dry skin mix with buttermilk. Thoroughly cleanse the face, apply the mask and relax for fifteen minutes. Rinse with tepid water and your skin will be delightfully soft and smooth.

Don't harm yourself by taking newfangled sleeping aids. A glass of warm milk or Ovaltine taken at bedtime will serve just as well. Grandma knew best, and sometimes added a teaspoon or two of brandy. Breathe deeply and relax your whole body; sleep will come, naturally.

An onion sandwich and a glass of hot milk just before retiring is a good cure for insomnia.

The humble carrot has curative properties — good for the outside as well as the inside. To cure winter sores suffered by the children as a result of long rides or walks to school and back, or by your husband after long hours in the paddocks, make this curing poultice. Scrape a large carrot, add a little sugar, and moisten with the top off the milk. Spread this on a clean piece of cloth, place over the sore and bandage securely. This will draw out the pus and clear the trouble in a day or so. The same poultice will clear boils and carbuncles.

It is a very thoughtful idea when writing to an incapacitated invalid friend to enclose a stamped addressed envelope and a sheet of paper for her to use for a reply.

Another tip for sleeplessness: the person who sleeps with a low pillow under the head and a plump one under the feet will rest far better than under the usual conditions.

One of Grandmother's favoured remedies was tea brewed from thyme. She would have prescribed this for jumpy nerves.

Here is a good laxative. The ingredients are half a pound of prunes, half a pound of brown sugar, three-quarters of an ounce of powdered senna and half an ounce of ground ginger. Soak prunes overnight in enough water to cover, then simmer until tender and add sugar. Take off the fire and rub through a sieve. Mix in ginger and senna (senna pods or powder can be bought at the chemist). Mix well together, put in jars. The dose is one teaspoon at night. Keeps well.

For fruit salts you will need eight ounces of icing sugar, four ounces of tartaric acid, one ounce of magnesia, four ounces of cream of tartar, four ounces of bicarb soda and four ounces of Epsom salts. Mix all together and sift several times (this is a dry mix). Put into glass jars and keep tightly covered. The dose is one teaspoon in a glass of water.

Make this gargle for sore throats and colds. Mix one cup of lukewarm water, one-and-a-half teaspoons of vinegar and a pinch of bicarb soda. Gargle frequently.

An arthritis potion. Fill a bottle with one-third each of sulphur, gin, and previously boiled cold water. Shake thoroughly. Take one eggcup full first thing in the morning. The quantity may be reduced according to need.

If you have an annoying cough which prevents sleep, take a pinch of salt. This never fails.

Beat an eggwhite to a stiff froth and whip with the juice of a small lemon. A teaspoon taken every hour will relieve hoarseness and coughing. If taking it every hour is too tedious, take at least six times a day, and especially at bedtime. A little honey can be added for children.

When the tongue is sore after eating pineapple or other acid fruits, smear bicarb soda on it, leave for a few seconds, then drink a glass of water.

A solution of one teaspoon of salt, one teaspoon of bicarb soda and a cup of lukewarm water will relieve swelling of the eyes caused by insect bites.

Here's how to make 'shoo-fly'. In a small bottle mix equal parts of vinegar and methylated spirits. This is good not only for mosquito bites but for other insect bites as well. Keep always on hand.

Mix equal parts of olive oil, sulphur and glycerine. This makes a good ointment for all cuts and sores.

If a mustard plaster is mixed with the white of an egg it will not cause a blister when applied.

Invalids resting out of doors or lying near an open window are often disturbed by pestering insects. To discourage them, put a square of camphor and half a dozen cloves in a muslin bag and fix to the head of the chair or bed. Insects don't like the odour.

Sir A. Clarke's method of making tea. Make the tea with boiling milk as you would with water. Scald the teapot, put in about one-and-a-half teaspoons of good tea for a cup and pour about half a pint of freshly boiled milk over it. Let it stand for three minutes and serve. This is excellent for an invalid or an aged person.

Try baked milk for an invalid. Sometimes when milk is disliked by the patient, a little served this way is palatable. Put one pint of milk into a greased pie dish and stand in a dish of water in a very slow oven for three to four hours. Some of the water in the milk evaporates; thus the quantity of the milk is reduced and it is creamy and deliciously flavoured.

If you have a sore or injured foot and the weight of the bedclothes causes you pain and distress, put the foot in a wastepaper basket and draw the bedcovers over the top. If children have a foot injury this will relieve the trauma and help to calm them.

If a sick-bed table is wanted and none is available, put the sewing machine alongside the bed and let the flap down over the bed. Makes a stable, solid surface.

For that lone morning cuppa when all the family have gone their way, use a gaily printed teatowel as a tablecloth. Good for the morale and sets you right for the day ahead.

Keep a small table in your bedroom for writing letters and planning menus. A chair with a padded seat, the table, a bowl of fresh flowers and peace all round are more conducive to good correspondence and thinking up delicious meals than balancing a writing pad on your knee or trying to choose a pudding in a hot kitchen. You need to be away from the work centre in order to relax.

Make yourself an 'illness trousseau' consisting of dainty nighties and bedjackets for the time you may need them. If you keep them wrapped in tissue paper with a perfumed sachet of lavender you will be prepared without any fuss if and when that hospital visit comes around.

When your new telephone book comes to hand, pass the old one over to a neighbour who has no telephone. She will find the directory very handy for addresses of firms she may want to contact by letter. Whatever you do, don't just throw it away.

A drop of any good perfume added to the inkwell gives a delightful fragrance to your written missive. A tiny spot of your favourite perfume dabbed on the corner of your stationery when sending a letter to loved ones brings you closer to them.

Grandma took this precaution. Avoid all possibility of error by writing the full date on any important documents instead of putting figures alone; for instance September 12, 1930, instead of 12/9/30. This method is proof against alteration by unscrupulous folk.

If you have received a letter which annoys you and calls for an angry reply, write it at once, but don't post it. Hold it until the morning, then read both the letter received and your reply. Reconsidering may save you many a heartache.